Contents

PS⎯⎯⎯⎯⎯Y

Clemson University

Drew Westen
Emory University

WILEY

JOHN WILEY & SONS, INC.

To order books or for customer service, please call 1-800-CALL-WILEY (225-5945).

ISBN 0-471-65039-0

Printed in the United States of America

10 9 8 7 6 5 4 3 2 1

Printed and bound by Courier Kendallville, Inc.

Preface
How to Use This Study Guide

Congratulations on having purchased the study guide to accompany **Psychology** *(4th edition)* by Robin Kowalski and Drew Westen. The purpose of this guide is to get you actively involved in learning the material in your textbook. Its goal is to help you better understand and apply the concepts from the book. Proper use of the study guide, therefore, will enhance your learning of psychology as it is delineated in this well-written textbook.

The study guide has been designed to facilitate *active* learning. For many students, learning and studying are all-too-often passive rather than active processes. Attending class, reading the textbook, and so on, are, of course, important parts of learning, but most of these activities place students in the role of passive recipient of knowledge rather than active participant in learning. Even when studying, many students simply reread what they have highlighted, recopy their notes, and so on. These strategies lack active integration of knowledge and diagnostic testing of information.

By contrast, active learning requires that students take control of the learning process. Taking control of the learning process means studying in a manner that facilitates *learning*, not superficial memorization. Specifically, actively learning psychology from your Kowalski and Westen textbook requires previewing your textbook to identify exactly where the book and the course are going, pre-reading each chapter before you read it so you can maximize your reading comprehension, working the chapter as opposed to simply reading it, reviewing what you have learned after you read a chapter, and testing your knowledge on an on-going basis so that it becomes committed to memory.

This study guide provides you with specific guidelines for previewing the textbook, pre-reading and working each chapter, and reviewing what you have learned. It also incorporates a variety of diagnostic exercises that will enable you to evaluate what you have learned and "zero in" on areas in which you need to improve. Finally, it outlines an effective method for exam preparation based on the knowledge you have garnered from working through this guide.

The following outline details exactly how to get the most out of this study guide and the Kowalski and Westen psychology text. Take the time to read through each point and incorporate the suggestions. Most of all, enjoy learning about psychology!

Preview The Textbook

How often have you skipped over all the introductory stuff in a textbook and instead started reading chapter one so you could "get to it." Believe it or not, there is a reason for all that introductory stuff, and skipping it makes learning the content of the book harder. Before you begin reading chapter one, take a little time to preview the book. Begin by reading the author's preface. It will tell you how the book is laid out, why it's laid out that way, and what to expect in each chapter.

Next, read the detailed table of contents so you can see what the author was talking about. Take out your course syllabus and compare it to the table of contents. How does your professor plan to use the textbook? Will you be covering one chapter per week, one chapter per class, or multiple chapters per class? Do you need to know a chapter inside-and-out before class so you can discuss it, or are you reading the textbook as supplemental material to topics covered in class? When will you be tested? Can you tell from the syllabus how many chapters are covered on an exam? Mark dates and as much information as you can on the table of contents so you know exactly when you need to do what.

Combine this information to create a "time line" of the semester. You may even wish to create a master calendar of all your courses, so you can determine crunch times, etc. Let's face it—in a perfect world, you would study as little as possible to learn as much as you can. Doing a little work up front will enable you to balance all the stuff you have going on, do well in your courses, and still have time for an occasional social activity.

Chapter By Chapter

There are three parts to actively learning each chapter. First, **pre-read and work** the chapter. Second, **review and learn** the content. Third, **test and know** the material.

Pre-read and Work

Why is it easier to read about a subject with which you are familiar than about a totally foreign topic? The more you know about something, the easier it is for your brain to process related information (after studying chapters 3-6, you'll know exactly why this is true). Therefore, to get the most out of your reading, you need to know—before you read it—what it's going to be about. If you read a chapter without having any idea what's going to be covered or what important information will show up, it will be easy to get lost in the details of the chapter and miss the salient points. Also, it is very difficult upon first read to comprehend complex material that's full of unfamiliar jargon. Therefore, to maximize your reading, pre-read each chapter so you recognize important stuff when you come to it.

How do you pre-read a chapter? First, open to the appropriate chapter in the book and corresponding study guide chapter. Carefully read the table of contents at the front of the chapter in the book. Then flip to the summary at the end of the chapter and carefully read each point. This will give you a good idea of the important points of this chapter . Although you won't remember all these points, you will recognize many of them when you read the chapter. This recognition will enhance your ability to assimilate the important information in the chapter more quickly.

Now you are ready to begin to "work" the first segment of the chapter. (Note: If a segment is long or covers particularly dense material, you may wish to read the author's interim summary before you read the segment). Working a segment means actively reading while keeping an eye on what you are trying to glean from the text. As you read, jot down your questions, comments, and notes in the space provided in the **Outline** section of the study guide, and make note of the important terms you come across. Include page numbers of and references to difficult material that you know you will need to review. After you have finished your reading, turn to the **Learning Objectives**. These objectives take the form of short-answer questions. After reading the chapter, check off the questions you are confident that you can answer well. Review the material in the textbook for the questions about which you are less confident, recording the important points from your reading in the space below each question.

Review and Learn

After you finish working a chapter, you need to take time to really learn the material. This cannot be done immediately after you read the chapter. If possible, wait a day and then review the content of the chapter you read. If you need to do it all in one night, take a break or do some other homework that is completely different from this text.

To review a chapter, reread your answers to the learning objectives questions and key terms, plus your notes. Flip back to any parts of the text about which you feel less-than-confident and reread them. Also, reread the author's interim summaries and end-of-chapter summaries. Mark any areas that seem difficult or confusing to you so you can review them again in the future.

Once you have reviewed the material, apply your knowledge *without referring back to the textbook*. Define the **Key Terms** and do the **Fill-in Exercises**. Then, do the **Application** and **Using What You Have Learned** exercises.

As you work, mark any of the terms or questions that give you difficulty. Once you have finished an exercise, go back to your notes to find answers to the questions that gave you trouble. If you need to, go back to the textbook to find the answers. Finally, check your terms by flipping through the textbook or reading the end-of-chapter summary. All the key terms in the study guide are in **bold** in the text, and are also listed at the end of each chapter in the text. Answers to the fill-ins are found in the answer key in the study guide.

Why should you find the answers to difficult questions on your own as opposed to checking the answer key? The idea of these exercises is to help you commit this information to memory, to really *learn* the content of the chapter. If you were to simply check your work against an answer key, you would not be actively learning. The more clear you are about *why* an answer is right, the more likely you are to understand and remember it. This goes for questions you answered correctly by virtue of a "lucky guess." If you guessed on a question, mark it as a guess and verify it by looking back to your notes and the textbook.

Test and Know

On a separate day (preferably after some period of time has lapsed), test yourself using the **Sample Questions**. You may wish to mark your answers on a separate sheet of paper, and take this test again before you have an exam in class (see "Exam Review Strategy" later in this chapter for more exam prep ideas). Again, when you check your answers, review the information thoroughly. Getting questions right is good; knowing why they are right is better.

Upon completing these three parts to active learning, the information contained in a chapter will be stuff you *know*, not stuff you have temporarily memorized for a test. As you work through subsequent chapters, go back and review parts of earlier chapters as needed. The chapters in your textbook build on each other, so reviewing earlier concepts will be easy. If you continually review the concepts you have learned, you won't need to "cram for the exam," because you will know most of the information cold. You may need to review complicated concepts and terms, but you shouldn't need to reread the basic stuff.

Sounds like an awful lot of work, right? Active learning does require more effort. However, imagine instead taking a passive approach to learning this stuff. You read the book. You highlight stuff. Midterms come and you have nine chapters (over 350 pages) of stuff to reread and relearn in one day to be ready for the exam, not to mention that you also have four other major courses to cram for and tickets to the concert of the year. Active learning requires more investment up front, but pays off big in the end. Given that you have to read the stuff anyway, why not take the time to learn it the first time?

Exam Review Strategy

If you have consistently worked with this study guide, exam preparation will involve:

- Testing yourself
- Reviewing your notes on each chapter
- Reviewing tricky terms
- Rereading difficult segments (previously indicated by you)
- Rereading the interim summaries and end-of-chapter summaries
- Testing yourself

First test how well you have learned the information by giving yourself a mini-exam. To create a mini-exam, rework the Key Terms, Learning Objectives, and Sample Questions for each chapter (cover your answers or have a friend ask you the questions).

Once you take the mini-exam, you will know exactly how much studying you need to do. Review and reread what you need to (for the most thorough review, follow the outline above). This review shouldn't take long since you've done all the pre-work. After you finish your review, take your mini-exam again, or have a classmate "quiz you" on stuff from the chapters in the textbook. Then, go ace that exam!

Hopefully you will find this study guide a useful tool which enables you to truly learn psychology as it is presented in your textbook. Good luck in your course. This is a great psychology text—enjoy learning about psychology!

Alastair Younger

Chapter 1
Psychology: The Study of Mental Processes and Behavior

PART ONE: PRE-READ AND WORK
Outline and Learning Objectives

Pre-read this chapter's table of contents and end-of-chapter summary. Then, use the outline segment-by-segment to help you work through the chapter. Jot down your own questions, comments, and notes in the space provided. Make a note of key terms and of difficult areas that you will need to review (include page numbers). Then, answer the questions in the learning objectives section that follows. Check off those you are confident that you can answer well. Re-read the material in the text for the questions about which you are less confident. Record the important points from your reading in the space below each question.

OUTLINE

The Boundaries and Borders of Psychology

From Brain to Behavior: The Boundary with Biology

A Global Vista: The Boundary with Culture

From Philosophy to Psychology

Perspectives in Psychology

The Psychodynamic Perspective

The Behaviorist Perspective

The Cognitive Perspective

The Evolutionary Perspective

The Big Picture Questions

LEARNING OBJECTIVES

Upon completion of Chapter 1, you should be able to answer the following questions.

1.   What is the issue of localization of function in the brain?

2.   What are the two types of aphasias described by Paul Broca and Carl Wernicke?

3.   What types of questions are studied by psychological anthropologists and cross-cultural psychologists?

4.   In what ways did functionalism differ from structuralism?

5.   What are the three key components of a paradigm?

6.   According to Kuhn, how do the social sciences differ from the natural sciences?

7.   Briefly describe the origins of the psychodynamic approach.

8.   What are the three key premises of the psychodynamic perspective?

9.   Briefly describe the methods and data of the psychodynamic perspective.

10.   Briefly describe the origins of the behaviorist approach.

11.   In what two ways does the behaviorist perspective differ from Descartes's philosophical perspective?

12.   How does the behaviorist view of the subject matter and research methods of psychology differ from that of the psychodynamic and structuralist schools of thought?

13.   What is the primary metaphor of behaviorism?

14.   Briefly describe the origins of the cognitive approach.

15.   How do cognitive psychologists employ the metaphor of the computer to understand and model the way the mind works?

16.   What are the similarities and differences between the behaviorist perspective and the cognitive perspective?

17.   Briefly describe the origins of the evolutionary perspective.

18.   Explain the fundamental principles of the evolutionary.

19.   Why have many psychologists from other perspectives challenged the research methods commonly used by evolutionary psychologists? How have the methods used by evolutionary psychologists changed in recent years?

20.   Outline the various subdisciplines of psychology and the types of questions asked by each.

21.   Discuss eight "Big Picture" philosophical questions that set the stage for psychology and are central to contemporary psychological theory and research.

PART TWO: REVIEW AND LEARN
Key Terms, Fill-In Exercises, Application and Using What You Have Learned

Before doing the exercises below, review the information you learned in this chapter. Reread the work you did in part one of this study guide chapter, plus the interim summaries and end-of-chapter summary in your textbook. Review any problem areas. Once you feel comfortable with the material, do the following exercises without referring to your notes or textbook. If you have difficulty with a term or question, mark it and come back to it. When you have finished an exercise, go back to your notes and the textbook to find the answers to the questions that gave you difficulty. Finally, check your answers (key terms against the textbook and the rest against the answer key).

KEY TERMS

Psychology   _____

_____

Biopsychology (or behavioral neuroscience)   _____

_____

Localization of function   _____

_____

Psychological anthropologists   _____

_____

Cross-cultural psychology   _____

_____

Free will versus determinism   _____

_____

Mind-body problem   _____

_____

Introspection   _____

_____

Structuralism   _____

_____

Functionalism   _____

_____

Paradigm   _____

_____

Perspectives   _____

_____

Psychodynamics   _____

_____

Psychodynamic perspective   _____

_____

Falsifiability criterion   _____

_____

Behaviorist (or behavioral) perspective   _____

_____

Behaviorism   _____

_____

Cartesian dualism   _____

_____

Cognition   _____

_____

Cognitive perspective   _____

_____

Information processing   _____

_____

Rationalist philosophers   _____

_____

Evolutionary perspective   _____

_____

Nature-nurture controversy   _____

_____

Natural selection   _____

_____

Adaptive traits   _____

_____

Ethology   _____

_____

Sociobiology   _____

_____

Evolutionary psychologists   _____

_____

Behavioral genetics   _____

_____

Reproductive success   _____

_____

Inclusive fitness _____

_____

Gestalt psychology   _____

_____

Empiricism   _____

_____

FILL-IN EXERCISES

Fill in the word or words that best fit in the spaces below.

1.   Wilhelm Wundt, often described as the _____ of psychology, emphasized a research method known as _____, in which trained subjects verbally reported everything that went through their minds when presented with a stimulus or task.

2.   Edward Tichener initiated an early school of thought known as _____ which hoped to devise a *periodic table* of the elements of human consciousness.

3.   A _____ is a broad system of theoretical assumptions that a scientific community uses to make sense of their domain of study.

4.   Freud argued that people have powerful _____ motives that underlie their conscious intentions.

5.   The psychodynamic perspective relies substantially on the _____-_____ method, which entails in-depth observation of a small number of people.

6.   The _____ criterion refers to the ability of a theory to be proven wrong as a means of advancing science.

7.   John Locke, the seventeenth century British philosopher, contended that at birth the mind is a _____ _____ upon which experience writes its story.

8.   Behaviorism focuses on the way objects or events in the environment, referred to as _____, come to control behavior through learning.

9.   Skinner observed that the behaviors of organisms can be controlled by environmental conditions that either _____ or _____ their likelihood of occurring.

10.   The primary method of behaviorism is the _____ method.

11.   Many cognitive psychologists use the metaphor of the _____ to understand and model the way the mind works. From this perspective, thinking is information processing.

12.   In contrast to the behaviorists, cognitive psychologists have shown _____ (*more/less*) interest in the questions raised by Descartes and other rationalist philosophers.

13.   As with behaviorism, the primary method of the cognitive perspective is _____, but with one important difference: Cognitive psychologists use such procedures to infer _____ processes at work.

14.   The degree to which inborn processes determine human behavior is a classic issue in psychology, called the _____-_____ controversy.

15.   The theory of natural selection suggests that natural forces select traits in organisms that are _____ and are likely to be passed on to their offspring.

16.   Organisms with fewer adaptive features for their particular _____, or environmental circumstance, are less likely to survive and reproduce.

17.   The fundamental concept in all contemporary evolutionary theories is that evolution selects traits that maximize organisms' _____ success.

18.   Conrad Lorenz hypothesized that jackdaws have a(n) _____ (i.e., inborn) tendency to become distressed whenever they see a creature dangling a black object resembling a jackdaw.

19.   According to _____ psychologists, perception is an active experience of imposing order on an overwhelming panorama or details by seeing them as parts of larger wholes.

20.   _____ refers to the belief that the road to scientific knowledge is systematic observation, and ideally experimental observation.

21.   The field of study that examines interactions of individual psychology and social phenomena is referred to as _____ psychology.

22.   The field of psychology that focuses on the nature and treatment of psychological processes that lead to emotional distress is referred to as _____ psychology.

USING WHAT YOU HAVE LEARNED

Chapter 1 presents four theoretical perspectives in psychology: psychodynamic, behaviorist, cognitive, and evolutionary. At first each seems to conflict with the others. Yet, as the author points out, often one approach complements another -- asks questions the other approach overlooks or adds information not addressed by the other approach. Spend some time reviewing each approach. Can you see their complementarity?

Try applying each approach to some aspect of your own life. Think, for example, about how you responded in a particular situation recently.

1.   Can you imagine the role of unconscious desires or attitudes, or some long forgotten conflict from your childhood (the psychodynamic perspective) influencing your behavior?

2.   What about prior experience? How do your experience with similar situations and the consequences associated with similar behavior (the behaviorist perspective) influence your current behavior?

3.   Consider how you interpret the circumstances surrounding your behavior, how others react to you, what you pay attention to in their reactions, and so on (the cognitive perspective).

4.   Finally, can you see any possible survival value in your behavior (the evolutionary perspective)? If not, could it be that this behavior might have been adaptive in a different niche?

APPLICATION

Consider the following explanations for anxiety. Which theory would be best associated with each explanation?

1.   At one point in time, anxiety was very adaptive, as it prepared us to either fight or flee from situations where real danger was present. In our current society, often neither fighting nor fleeing is a viable option.

2.   Anxiety comes about because certain environmental stimuli have been associated with negative or harmful consequences. The stimulus, therefore, comes to trigger an automatic fear response.

3.   Anxiety comes about because we develop negative expectations about what will likely happen in a particular situation. These expectations cause us to pay close attention to signs of potential harm and to process such information more easily than other information around us.

4.   Anxiety may come about from wishes or fears that we have put out of conscious awareness. We may not even be aware of why we are anxious.

PART THREE: TEST AND KNOW
SAMPLE TEST QUESTIONS

Test how well you have learned this chapter's material by answering the sample test questions. You may wish to mark your answers on a separate sheet of paper so you can reuse this test for exam review. Once you have completed the exam, check your answers and then go back to your notes and the textbook to review questions you found difficult.

1.   To understand an individual at a given point in time, psychologists must track

    a.   biological events
    b.   psychological experience
    c.   the cultural and historical context
    d.   all of the above

2.   Paul Broca observed that individuals with lesions in the front section of the left hemisphere

    a.   were able to speak fluently but could not comprehend language
    b.   were often unable to speak fluently but could comprehend language
    c.   could both speak fluently and comprehend well
    d.   were unable to comprehend language or speak comprehensibly

3.   Cross-cultural psychologists

    a.   attempt to distinguish universal psychological processes from those that are specific to particular cultures.
    b.   argue that the only important findings concerning psychological processes are those that hold true across cultures.
    c.   believe that all psychological processes are culturally specific; nothing is universal.
    d.   assert that all psychological processes involve an equal balance between the individual and his or her culture.

4.   "Do we freely choose our actions, or is our behavior caused by things outside our control?" This philosophical view is know as

    a.   rationalism versus empiricism
    b.   individualism versus relationality
    c.   free will versus determinism
    d.   nature versus nurture

5.   Whereas Edward Tichener was associated with the structuralist school of psychology, William James was a _____.

    a.   Gestalt psychologist
    b.   functionalist
    c.   psychoanalyst
    d.   behaviorist

6.   Which of the following is not a key component of a paradigm?

    a.   It includes a set of findings that will be considered acceptable by the scientific community.
    b.   It includes a set of theoretical assertions that provide a model of the object of study.
    c.   It includes a set of shared metaphors that compare the object under investigation to something else that is readily apprehended.
    d.   It includes a set of methods that members of the scientific community agree will, if properly executed, provide valid and useful data.

7. According to Kuhn, the social sciences differ from the older natural sciences in that

    a. social sciences lack an accepted paradigm upon which most members of the scientific community agree
    b. although they have an accepted paradigm upon which most members of the scientific community agree, social scientists tend to align themselves with one of several different perspectives
    c. there are a limited number of perspectives in the social sciences, whereas the number in the natural sciences seems unlimited
    d. social sciences borrow perspectives from the natural sciences, whereas the natural sciences never borrow from the social sciences

8. The relationship between conscious awareness and unconscious mental forces can be considered analogous to the visible tip of an iceberg and the vast, submerged hulk that lies out of sight beneath the water. This notion best fits with which of the following perspectives?

    a. psychodynamic
    b. behaviorist
    c. cognitive
    d. evolutionary

9. Which of the following research methods is most associated with the psychodynamic perspective?

    a. experimentation
    b. introspection
    c. case study
    d. observation

10. The notion that the mind at birth can be considered a "tabula rasa" is attributable to

    a. John Locke
    b. B. F. Skinner
    c. Ivan Pavlov
    d. René Descartes

11. Behaviorists argued that

    a. behavior must be considered in the context of motives and goals
    b. behavior can be understood entirely without reference to thoughts and feelings
    c. the science of psychology must emphasize the role of psychological processes in helping individuals adapt to their environment
    d. researchers should apply direct observational methods when studying the structure of consciousness

12.   The notion that humans and animals are like machines is the metaphor associated with which view?

a.   information processing
b.   structuralism
c.   psychodynamic
d.   behavioral

13.   The primary method of the behaviorist approach is

a.   introspection
b.   experimentation
c.   deduction
d.   determinism

14.   The notion of *information processing* is most associated with which perspective?

a.   evolutionary
b.   structuralist
c.   cognitive
d.   behaviorist

15.   The primary method of the cognitive perspective is

a.   introspection
b.   deduction
c.   case study
d.   experimentation

16.   Many, if not most, psychological processes

a.   are predominantly attributable to environmental influences
b.   reflect predominantly the influence of innate, biological processes
c.   reflect an interaction between nature and nurture
d.   are primarily learned, and not biologically ordained

17.   The field of science that studies animal behavior from a biological and evolutionary perspective is

a.   sociobiology
b.   ethology
c.   behavioral genetics
d.   anthropological psychology

18. Behavioral genetics

    a. refers to an organism's capacity to survive and produce offspring
    b. is the study of animal behavior from a biological and evolutionary perspective
    c. explores possible evolutionary and biological bases of human social behavior
    d. examines the genetic and environmental bases of differences among individuals on psychological traits

19. Psychologists interested in such phenomena as prejudice, aggression, and groups would most likely be classified as _____ psychologists.

    a. clinical
    b. health
    c. industrial/organizational
    d. social

20. The notion that perception involves imposing order on an overwhelming panorama of details by seeing them as parts of larger wholes, was held by

    a. the structuralists
    b. psychodynamic psychologists
    c. Gestalt psychologists
    d. the functionalists

Answers

Fill-in Exercises

1. father; introspection   2. structuralism   3. paradigm   4. unconscious   5. case-study   6. falsifiability
7. tabula rasa   8. stimuli   9. increase (reinforce); decrease (punish)   10. experimental   11. computer
12. more   13. experimental; mental   14. nature-nurture   15. adaptive   16. niche   17. reproductive
18. innate   19. Gestalt   20. empiricism   21. social   22. clinical

Application

1. Evolutionary perspective
2. Behaviorist perspective
3. Cognitive perspective
4. Psychodynamic perspective

Sample Test Questions

1.	d	11.	b
2.	b	12.	d
3.	a	13.	b
4.	c	14.	c
5.	b	15.	d
6.	a	16.	c
7.	a	17.	b
8.	a	18.	d
9.	c	19.	d
10.	a	20.	c

Chapter 2
Research Methods in Psychology

PART ONE: PRE-READ AND WORK
Outline and Learning Objectives

Pre-read this chapter's table of contents and end-of-chapter summary. Then, use the outline segment-by-segment to help you work through the chapter. Jot down your own questions, comments, and notes in the space provided. Make a note of key terms and of difficult areas that you will need to review (include page numbers). Then, answer the questions in the learning objectives section that follows. Check off those you are confident that you can answer well. Re-read the material in the text for the questions about which you are less confident. Record the important points from your reading in the space below each question.

OUTLINE

Characteristics of Good Psychological Research

Theoretical Framework

Focus on Methodology: Getting Research Ideas

Standardized Procedures

Generalizability from a Sample

Objective Measurement

Descriptive Research

Case Study Methods

Naturalistic Observation

Survey Research

Focus on Methodology: What to Do with Descriptive Research

Experimental Research

The Logic Of Experimentation

Steps in Conducting an Experiment

Limitations of Experimental Research

Focus on Methodology: Testing the Hypothesis – Inferential Statistics

Correlational Research

From Brain to Behavior: Researching the Brain

A Global Vista: Cross-Cultural Research

How to Evaluate a Study Critically

One Step Further: Ethical Questions Come in Shades of Gray

LEARNING OBJECTIVES

Upon completion of Chapter 2, you should be able to answer the following questions.

1.   What are the major characteristics of good psychological research?

2.   What are a theory, a hypothesis, and a variable and how are they related?

3.   Differentiate between the internal and external validity of a study.

4.   What is meant by the *reliability* of a measure? Describe three important kinds of reliability.

5.   How do researchers ensure the *validity* of a psychological measure? Describe three types of validity.

6.   Why are multiple measures important to obtain an accurate assessment of a variable?

7.   What are the advantages and limitations of each of the following descriptive methods?

Case study

Naturalistic observation

Survey research

8.   How do researchers using the survey method ensure that their sample reflects the demographic characteristics of the population of interest?

9.   What are the similarities and differences between the mean and the mode?

10.   What are two methods of measuring variability?

11.   How do experimental methods allow researchers to assess cause-and-effect relations between variables?

12.   How do independent and dependent variables differ?

13.   What are the six steps involved in conceiving and executing an experiment?

14.   Why are control groups important in experimental research?

15.   What is the purpose of *blind* studies in experimental research? How do *double-blind* studies differ from *single-blind* studies?

16.   Why is random assignment important in experimental research?

17.   What are two limitations of experimental research?

18.   How are descriptive statistics and inferential statistics used?

19.   What is a quasi-experimental design and why do researchers use such designs?

20.   How do correlation coefficients represent the relation between variables? What is the difference between positive and negative correlations?

21.   What is meant by the phrase "correlation does not imply causation"?

22.   Compare the following methods researchers use to study the brain:

        Electroencephalogram (EEG)

        Computerized axial tomography (CT-scan)

        Magnetic resonance imaging (MRI)

        Positron emission tomography (PET)

        Functional magnetic resonance imaging (fMRI).

23.   What difficulties do researchers face when trying to transport research from one culture to another?

24.   What are seven important criteria that can be used to evaluate a study critically?

25.   What four conditions must be met before deception can be used in a study?

26.   Discuss the ethical controversy concerning the use of animals in psychological research.

PART TWO: REVIEW AND LEARN
Key Terms, Fill-In Exercises, Application and Using What You Have Learned

Before doing the exercises below, review the information you learned in this chapter. Reread the work you did in part one of this study guide chapter, plus the interim summaries and end-of-chapter summary in your textbook. Review any problem areas. Once you feel comfortable with the material, do the following exercises without referring to your notes or textbook. If you have difficulty with a term or question, mark it and come back to it. When you have finished an exercise, go back to your notes and the textbook to find the answers to the questions that gave you difficulty. Finally, check your answers (key terms against the textbook and the rest against the answer key).

KEY TERMS

Theory _____

_____

Hypothesis   _____

_____

Variable   _____

_____

Continuous variable   _____

_____

Categorical variable   _____

_____

Standardized procedures _____

_____

Population _____

_____

Sample _____

_____

Representative _____

_____

Participants (or Subjects) _____

_____

Generalizability _____

_____

Valid _____

_____

Internal validity _____

_____

External validity _____

_____

Experimenter's dilemma _____

_____

Measure _____

_____

Reliability _____

_____

Test-retest reliability _____

_____

Internal consistency _____

_____

Interrater reliability _____

_____

Validity _____

_____

Face validity _____

_____

Construct validity _____

_____

Criterion validity _____

_____

Error _____

_____

Descriptive research _____

_____

Case study _____

_____

Naturalistic observation _____

_____

Survey research_____

_____

Interviews _____

_____

Questionnaires _____

_____

Random sample_____

_____

Stratified random sample _____

_____

Mean _____

_____

Mode _____

_____

Variability _____

_____

Range _____

_____

Standard deviation _____

_____

Experimental research _____

_____

Independent variables _____

_____

Dependent variables _____

_____

Conditions _____

_____

Operationalizing _____

_____

Control group _____

_____

Demand characteristics _____

_____

Blind studies _____

_____

Placebo effect _____

_____

Single-blind study _____

_____

Double-blind study _____

_____

Confounding variable   _____

_____

Descriptive statistics   _____

_____

Inferential statistics   _____

_____

Quasi-experimental designs   _____

_____

Probability value (or *p*-value)   _____

_____

Correlational research   _____

_____

Correlate   _____

_____

Correlation coefficient   _____

_____

Positive correlation   _____

_____

Negative correlation   _____

_____

Correlation matrix   _____

_____

Electroencephalogram (EEG) _____

_____

Neuroimaging techniques   _____

_____

Computerized axial tomography (CT scan or CAT scan) _____

_____

Magnetic resonance imaging (MRI)   _____

_____

Positron emission tomography (PET)   _____

_____

Functional magnetic resonance imaging (fMRI) _____

_____

Informed consent   _____

_____

FILL-IN EXERCISES

Fill in the word or words that best fit in the spaces below.

1. A _____ is a tentative belief about the relationship between two or more variables.

2. A variable is any phenomenon that can _____ from one situation to another or from one person to another.

3. A variable that can be placed on a continuum is a _____ variable, whereas one comprised of groupings or categories is a _____ variable.

4. The individuals who take part in a study are referred to as _____.

5. A _____ is a subgroup of the population that is likely to be _____ of the population as a whole – that is, similar enough to the population to allow conclusions to de drawn about the rest of the population.

6. If the findings of a study can be generalized to situations outside the laboratory, the study has established _____ _____.

7. Three kinds of reliability are especially important: _____ reliability refers to the ability of a test to yield relatively similar scores for the same individual over time. _____ consistency or _____ reliability refers to the consistency of participants' responses across items on a scale. Finally, _____ reliability refers to the similarity of ratings by two different interviewers of the same individual on the same dimension.

8. _____ validity refers to the degree to which a measure actually assesses what it claims to measure to assess, while _____ validity refers to the degree to which a measure allows a researcher to distinguish among groups on the basis of certain behaviors or responses.

9. Because every measure includes some degree of error, investigators often employ _____ measures of the variable.

10. Psychologists who take an *interpretive* (or *hermeneutic*) approach to methodology often use _____ studies; their aim is to examine the complex meanings that may underlie human behavior.

11. When using naturalistic observation, researchers often use one of two ways to minimize participants' awareness of being watched. One way is simply to be as _____ as possible. The other is to become a _____-_____, interacting naturally with subjects in their environment.

12. The two most frequently used tools of survey researchers are _____ and _____.

13.   When using survey methods, sometimes proportional representation of different subpopulations is important to researchers. A _____ random sample specifies the percentage of participants to be drawn from each population category and then _____ selects from within each category.

14.   Several common measures of central tendency often employed by researchers: The _____ is the statistical average of the scores of all participants. The _____ refers to the most common score observed in the sample. The _____ of scores refers to how much participants' scores differ from one another.

15.   Using experimental methods allows researchers to directly establish _____-and-_____ relations between variables.

16.   In an experiment, the experimenter manipulates the _____ variable and measures the _____ variable to see if the experimental manipulation had an effect.

17.   Turning an abstract concept into a concrete variable is called _____ the variable.

18.   To ensure that the only things that vary from participant to participant are the independent variables and the participants' performance on the dependent variables, investigators develop a _____ procedure for all participants.

19.   Instead of being exposed to the experimental manipulation, individuals in the _____ group experience a neutral condition.

20.   _____ _____ are cues in the experimental situation that can reveal the experimenter's purpose.

21.   Simply believing that a treatment is effective can sometimes prove as effective as the treatment itself, a phenomenon called the _____ effect.

22.   A _____-_____ study is a way of reducing the effects of the biases of both participants and researchers.

23.   A _____ variable can produce effects that are confused with the effects of the independent variable, which can compromise the internal validity of the study.

24.   In analyzing the findings of a study, _____ statistics are used to summarize the essential features of the data, whereas _____ statistics are used to draw inferences from the sample studied to the population as a whole.

25.   An advantage of experiments is that they can be _____ -- that is, repeated to see if the same findings emerge with a different sample.

26.   To _____ two variables means to assess the extent to which being high or low on one measure predicts being high or low on the other.

27.   The _____ measures the electrical activity toward the surface of the brain.

28.   The _____ _____ is a neuroimaging technique that involves analyzing the results of a series of X-ray pictures taken as a scanner rotates about a person's head.

USING WHAT YOU HAVE LEARNED

In Chapter 2, you learned about different research methods that are used in psychology. Below you will find the names of various research methods. Identify which method best describes each of the examples of research studies that follow.

Research Methods

Naturalistic observation   Case study
Survey research   Correlational research
Quasi-experiment   Experimental research

Studies

1.   The relation between college students' final exam grades and the number of hours they spent studying for the exam is examined.

2.   A psychology professor wants to determine whether showing videotapes as an adjunct to his lectures improves students' performance. He randomly creates two groups of students: those in one group watch videotapes that illustrate the material in the lecture, while those in the other just attend the lectures (no tapes). He then compares their grades on the exam.

3.   A researcher is interested in whether there are gender differences in grades in the Introduction to psychology course. She compares the grades of the female students to those of the male students in the course.

4.   At the end of each semester, the university asks students to complete a questionnaire evaluating the course they are taking and the professor who teaches it. The information is used to provide feedback to the department and to the professors concerning both course content and teaching methods.

5.   A team of developmental psychologists, interested in the phenomenon of bullying, spends several weeks observing children at recess and lunch break in their school playground.

6.   A clinical psychologist collects considerable information concerning each patient that he sees, including information concerning his or her childhood (family and school experiences), job and career, romantic relationships, and so on. His goal is to put together a comprehensive picture of each patient.

APPLICATION

Situation

A researcher is interested in whether taking vitamin C has an effect on the number of colds people get.

Questions to Answer

1.   If she wants to determine whether taking vitamin C actually reduces the number of colds people get (i.e., a cause-and-effect relationship), what type of research procedure should she use?

2.   What procedures would she follow in setting up such a study?

3.   What could she select for the independent and dependent variables?

4.   Do you think a control group would be important? Why? What kind of neutral condition could she use with a control group?

5.   How could she control for possible demand characteristics in the study?

PART THREE: TEST AND KNOW
SAMPLE TEST QUESTIONS

Test how well you have learned this chapter's material by answering the sample test questions. You may wish to mark your answers on a separate sheet of paper so you can reuse this test for exam review. Once you have completed the exam, check your answers and then go back to your notes and the textbook to review questions you found difficult.

1.   A systematic way to organize and explain observations, which includes a set of propositions or statements about the relations among various phenomena is a

a.	hypothesis	b.	paradigm
c.	theory	d.	model

2.   The term _____ refers to the applicability of a study's findings to the entire population of interest to the researchers.

a.	internal validity	b.	generalizability
c.	reliability	d.	internal consistency

3.   If several ways of asking the same question yield similar results, a measure has

a.	retest reliability	b.	internal consistency
c.	interrater reliability	d.	internal validity

4.   Because case study research gains its insights from examining only one participant, generalization to a larger population is always uncertain. One way to minimize this limitation is to

   a.   use a multiple-case-study approach
   b.   use a control group
   c.   employ double-blind case study designs
   d.   stop trying to generalize

5.   A researcher is interested in whether watching "Sesame Street" on TV has a positive impact on children's grades at school. She records the number of days children watch "Sesame Street" over a one-month interval and relates it to their grades on their report cards at school. This study is best described as

   a.   experimental
   b.   quasi-experimental
   c.   a survey
   d.   correlational

6.   The major problem with survey methods is the following:

   a.   It is often difficult to get participants to participate in this kind of study.
   b.   They rely on participants to report on themselves truthfully and accurately.
   c.   It is questionable whether the results can be generalized to the larger population.
   d.   It is often difficult to keep participants unaware of the purpose of the study and thus demand characteristics can be a major concern.

7.   A measure of variability that is more useful than the *range* is the

   a.   histogram   b.   normal distribution
   c.   central tendency   d.   standard deviation

8.   In an experiment, the investigator can determine whether a _____ relation exists between two variables, whereas this cannot be determined in a study using correlational methods.

   a.   valid
   b.   cause-and-effect
   c.   generalizable
   d   reliable

9.   Operationalizing the variable involves

   a.   turning an abstract concept into a concrete variable
   b.   predicting the relation between two or more variables
   c.   putting your research plan into operation
   d.   manipulating a variable and observing the operation of its effects

10.   A researcher has developed a new treatment for smoking which combines hypnosis and acupuncture. He randomly creates two groups of participants and administers his new treatment to one group, while the other group receives no treatment. He measures the number of cigarettes participants smoke in the two weeks following treatment. This study is best described as

a.   descriptive   b.   correlational
c.   quasi-experimental   d.   experimental

11.   What is the dependent variable in the above example?

a.   the two groups of participants
b.   the 2 weeks following treatment
c.   hypnosis and acupuncture
d.   the number of cigarettes smoked

12.   In the above example, it would be important for the researchers to ensure that participants are kept unaware of the goals of the research; otherwise, their behavior might be affected. To do so, the researcher would conduct

a.   a single-blind study
b.   a. quasi-experimental study
c.   a case study
d.   a correlational study

13.   In the above example, if participants in the treatment condition were older than those in the no-treatment condition, age would be a(n) _____ variable.

a.   independent   b.   dependent
c.   confounding   d.   correlational

14.   Tests of statistical significance determine

a.   whether the results of a study are high in practical significance
b.   whether the results of a study are high in theoretical significance
c.   whether the results of a study are likely to have occurred simply by chance
d.   whether the results of a study apply to situations outside the lab in which the research took place

15.   The number that indicates the direction and strength of the relation between two variables is referred to as a

a.   correlation coefficient
b.   correlation matrix
c.   scatter plot
d.   correlation plot

16. Assume an investigator has found a positive correlation between the number of aspirins people take and the number of headaches they get. The investigator could conclude the following from this correlation:

    a. Number of aspirins taken and number of headaches suffered are related to one another.
    b. People who take aspirin frequently seem to get fewer headaches.
    c. Taking aspirin causes people to have fewer headaches.
    d. Taking aspirin seems unrelated to whether people have headaches or not.

17. A hypothetical study of the relation between TV violence and aggressive behavior in children reveals a correlation of +.85 between the number of violent shows watched each week and children's level of aggressiveness. Based on these findings, which of the following conclusions might be true?

    a. Watching violent TV leads to aggressive behavior in children.
    b. Parents who do not allow their children to watch violent shows may discourage aggressive behavior in their children in other ways as well.
    c. Children who are more aggressive may have more of a "taste" for violent shows than those who are less aggressive.
    d. In fact, ALL of the above conclusions *could* be true.

18. A correlation of zero means that

    a. as the first variable increases, the other decreases
    b. as the first variable decreases, the other increases
    c. two variables are unrelated
    d. participants tended to score around zero on both variables

19. A procedure in which radioactive glucose is injected into the bloodstream allowing researchers to observe the brain in action is called

    a. an electroencephalogram (EEG)
    b. computerized axial tomography (CT scan)
    c. positron emission tomography (PET)
    d. magnetic resonance imaging (MRI)

20. When deception is used in research, researchers must be sure to

    a. pay the participants
    b. debrief the participants afterward
    c. instruct the participants not to talk about the true purposes of the study
    d. ensure that participants do not deduce the true purpose of the study, which could cause demand characteristics to bias the results

ANSWERS
FILL-IN EXERCISES

1. hypothesis   2. differ (or vary)   3. continuous; categorical   4. participants (or subjects)   5. sample; representative   6. external validity 7. test-retest; internal, inter-item; interrater 8. construct; criterion 9. multiple 10. case 11. inconspicuous; participant-observer 12. questionnaires; interviews 13. stratified; randomly 14. mean; mode; variability 15. cause; effect 16. independent; dependent 17. operationalizing 18. standardized 19. control   20. demand characteristics   21. placebo 22. double-blind 23. confounding 24. descriptive; inferential 25. replicated 26. correlate 27.electroencephalogram (EEG)   28. CT (or CAT) scan

USING WHAT YOU HAVE LEARNED

1. correlational research 2. experimental research 3. quasi-experiment 4. survey research 5. naturalistic observation 6. case study

APPLICATION

1. Experimental research
2. Follow the six steps of conceiving and executing an experiment: frame hypothesis; operationalize variables; develop standardized procedures; select and assign participants to conditions; apply statistical techniques to the results; and draw conclusions.
3. Independent variable -- level of vitamin C administered to each group (e.g., 0 mg/day; 100 mg/day; 500 mg/day);
Dependent variable -- number of colds participants in each group report during the duration of the study.
4. Yes; because of placebo effects. Use a placebo control (e.g., an inert pill).
5. Use a blind study (single-blind to control for demand characteristics; double blind to control as well for experimenter bias).

SAMPLE TEST QUESTIONS

1.	c	11.	d
2.	b	12.	a
3.	b	13.	c
4.	a	14.	c
5.	d	15.	a
6.	b	16.	a
7.	d	17.	d
8.	b	18.	c
9.	a	19.	c
10.	d	20.	b

Chapter 3
Biological Bases
of Mental Life and Behavior

PART ONE: PRE-READ AND WORK
Outline and Learning Objectives

Pre-read this chapter's table of contents and end-of-chapter summary. Then, use the outline segment-by-segment to help you work through the chapter. Jot down your own questions, comments, and notes in the space provided. Make a note of key terms and of difficult areas that you will need to review (include page numbers). Then, answer the questions in the learning objectives section that follows. Check off those you are confident that you can answer well. Re-read the material in the text for the questions about which you are less confident. Record the important points from your reading in the space below each question.

OUTLINE

Neurons: Basic Units of the Nervous System

Anatomy of a Neuron

Firing of a Neuron

Transmission of Information Between Cells

The Endocrine System

From Brain to Behavior: Psychoneuroimmunology

The Peripheral Nervous System

The Somatic Nervous System

The Autonomic Nervous System

The Central Nervous System

The Spinal Cord

The Hindbrain

The Midbrain

The Subcortical Forebrain

The Cerebral Cortex

A Global Vista: Environment, Culture, and the Brain

Genetics and Evolution

The Influence of Genetics on Psychological Functioning

Behavioral Genetics

A Global Vista: Genetic Homogeneity

Evolution

Evolution of The Central Nervous System

The Future: Genetic Engineering

LEARNING OBJECTIVES

Upon completion of Chapter 3, you should be able to answer the following questions.

1.   What are three kinds of neurons and what are their functions?

2.   What are the functions of the dendrites, the cell body, and the axon?

3.   Why is myelination important for the transmission of nerve impulses?

4.   How do graded potentials differ from action potentials?

5.   How are sodium and potassium ions involved in the transmission of an impulse down the axon?

6.   How do neurons communicate chemically with other neurons?

7.   How do excitatory and inhibitory neurotransmitters differ?

8.   What are the psychological functions of the following neurotransmitters?

Glutamate

GABA (Gamma-aminobutyric acid)

Dopamine

Serotonin

Acetylcholine (Ach)

Endorphins

9.   What is Parkinson's disease and what role does dopamine play in this disease?

10.   What are the functions of the following endocrine glands?

Pituitary gland

Thyroid gland

Adrenal glands

Gonads

11.   How does the nervous system affect the immune system?

12.   What are the major divisions of the nervous system?

13.   In what ways do the functions of the sympathetic nervous system and the parasympathetic nervous system differ?

14.   What is the major function of each of the following areas of the hindbrain?

Medulla oblongata

Reticular activating system

Cerebellum

15.   What are the major functions of the areas of the midbrain called the tectum and tegmentum?

16.   What is the major function of each of the following areas of the subcortical forebrain?

Hypothalamus

Thalamus

Limbic System

Basal ganglia

17.   What are three functions performed by the cerebral cortex?

18.   How do functions of the primary and association areas of the cerebral cortex differ?

19.   What are the major functions of each of the following four lobes of the cerebral cortex?

   Occipital

   Parietal

   Frontal

   Temporal

20.   How is space allocated to different parts of the body in the motor and somatosensory cortexes?

21.   What are the results of damage to Broca's and Wernicke's areas?

22.   What is meant by cerebral lateralization? List the various functions for which the left and right hemisphere are dominant.

23.   How does split-brain research provide evidence for cerebral lateralization?

24.   What cognitive differences have been found between females and males? What evidence is there for biological explanations for these differences?

25.   How are the effects of dominant and recessive alleles transmitted from parents to children?

26.   What are the differences between monozygotic and dizygotic twins?

27.   How do researchers assess the heritability of various characteristics?

28.   What evidence is there that certain information-processing modules designed to solve a certain problem of adaptation may be innate?

29.   How can the design of the central nervous system be considered to reflect its evolution?

PART TWO: REVIEW AND LEARN
Key Terms, Fill-In Exercises, Application and Using What You Have Learned

Before doing the exercises below, review the information you learned in this chapter. Reread the work you did in part one of this study guide chapter, plus the interim summaries and end-of-chapter summary in your textbook. Review any problem areas. Once you feel comfortable with the material, do the following exercises without referring to your notes or textbook. If you have difficulty with a term or question, mark it and come back to it. When you have finished an exercise, go back to your notes and the textbook to find the answers to the questions that gave you difficulty. Finally, check your answers (key terms against the textbook and the rest against the answer key).

KEY TERMS

Nervous system _____

_____

Neuron _____

_____

Sensory neurons _____

_____

Motor neurons _____

_____

Interneurons _____

_____

Dendrites   _____

_____

Cell body   _____

_____

Axon   _____

_____

Myelin sheath   _____

_____

Glial cells   _____

_____

Terminal buttons   _____

_____

Synapses_____

_____

Resting potential   _____

_____

Graded potentials   _____

_____

Action potentials   _____

_____

Neurotransmitters   _____

_____

Receptors   _____

_____

Glutamate   _____

_____

GABA   _____

_____

Dopamine   _____

_____

Parkinson's disease   _____

_____

Serotonin   _____

_____

Acetylcholine (Ach)   _____

_____

Endorphins   _____

_____

Endocrine system   _____

_____

Hormones   _____

_____

Adrenalin and noradrenalin   _____

_____

Pituitary gland _____

_____

Thyroid gland _____

_____

Adrenal glands _____

_____

Gonads _____

_____

Testosterone _____

_____

Estrogens _____

_____

Psychoneuroimmunology _____

_____

Central nervous system (CNS) _____

_____

Peripheral nervous system (PNS) _____

_____

Somatic nervous system _____

_____

Autonomic nervous system (ANS) _____

_____

Sympathetic nervous system   _____

_____

Parasympathetic nervous system   _____

_____

Spinal cord   _____

_____

Hindbrain   _____

_____

Medulla oblongata   _____

_____

Reticular activating system   _____

_____

Cerebellum   _____

_____

Midbrain   _____

_____

Tectum _____

_____

Tegmentum   _____

_____

Subcortical forebrain   _____

_____

Hypothalamus _____

_____

Thalamus _____

_____

Limbic system _____

_____

Amygdala _____

_____

Hippocampus _____

_____

Basal ganglia _____

_____

Cerebral cortex _____

_____

Primary areas _____

_____

Association areas _____

_____

Cerebral hemispheres _____

_____

Corpus callosum _____

_____

Occipital lobes _____

_____

Parietal lobes _____

_____

Somatosensory cortex _____

_____

Frontal lobes _____

_____

Motor cortex _____

_____

Broca's area _____

_____

Temporal lobes _____

_____

Wernicke's area _____

_____

Cerebral lateralization _____

_____

Split-brain _____

_____

Gene _____

_____

Chromosomes _____

_____

Alleles _____

_____

Homozygous _____

_____

Heterozygous _____

_____

Incomplete dominance _____

_____

Linkage studies _____

_____

Degree of relatedness _____

_____

Monozygotic (MZ) twins _____

_____

Dizygotic (DZ) twins _____

_____

Heritability coefficient _____

_____

Heritability _____

_____

Speciation _____

_____

Evolution _____

_____

Stigmatization _____

_____

Language Acquisition Device _____

_____

Reflexes _____

_____

Cerebrum _____

_____

FILL-IN EXERCISES

Fill in the word or words that best fit in the spaces below.

1.   _____ neurons transmit information from receptors to the brain. _____ neurons transmit information to the glands and muscles of the body.

2.   Branch-like extensions of the neuron, called _____, receive inputs from other neurons. If a neuron receives enough stimulation, it passes information to other neurons through its _____.

3.   The _____ matter of the brain is composed of myelinated _____.

4.   Multiple sclerosis is a disease in which the _____ sheath on large clusters of neurons degenerates, causing jerky, uncoordinated movement.

5.   At the end of an axon are terminal _____, which send signals from a neuron to adjacent cells.

6.   Connections between neurons occur at _____.

7.   An _____ (*increase/decrease*) in polarization inhibits the neuron, making it less likely to fire.

8.   The shift in polarity across the membrane and subsequent restoration of the resting potential is called a(n) _____ _____, or the "firing" of the neuron.

9.   _____ are chemicals that transmit information from one cell to another.

10.   _____ neurotransmitters depolarize the postsynaptic cell membrane, making an action potential more likely. In contrast, _____ neurotransmitters hyperpolarize the membrane, reducing the likelihood that the postsynaptic neuron will fire.

11.   Glutamate is a neurotransmitter that can _____ (*excite/inhibit*) nearly every neuron in the nervous system, whereas GABA is a neurotransmitter that plays an _____ (*excitatory/inhibitory*) role.

12.   Dopamine is synthesized by a part of the brain called the _____ _____, or "black substance."

13.   The neurotransmitter _____ is involved in learning and memory.

14.   The hormone adrenalin is the same compound as the neurotransmitter _____.

15.   The _____ gland is often described as the *"master gland"* because many of the hormones it releases stimulate and regulate the other glands.

16.   The _____ gland releases hormones that control growth and metabolism.

17.   The male gonads, referred to as _____, produce the hormone _____. The female gonads, referred to as _____, produce the hormone _____.

18.   _____ is the study of the interactions among behavior, the nervous system, the endocrine system, and the immune system.

19.   The _____ nervous system, because it is involved in intentional actions, is sometimes also called the voluntary nervous system.

20.   The _____ nervous system is typically activated in response to threats.

21.   The _____ _____ sends information from sensory neurons in various parts of the body to the brain, and it relays motor commands back to muscles and organs..

22.   The _____ is the area of the hindbrain involved in movement and fine motor learning, as well as other functions.

23.   Damage to the _____ _____ system in the hindbrain is a major cause of coma.

24. The _____ is a set of nuclei located above the hypothalamus in the subcortical forebrain. One of its most important functions is to process sensory information as it arrives and transmit this information to higher brain centers.

25. The _____ system is a set of structures in the subcortical forebrain with diverse functions involving emotion, motivation, learning, and memory.

26. The hills and valleys making up the convolutions of the cortex are referred to as _____ and _____, respectively.

27. The _____ areas of the cortex process raw sensory information or initiate motor movements, while the _____ areas are involved in constructing perceptions, ideas, and plans.

28. The _____ lobes of the cortex are involved in the sense of touch, detecting movement in the environment, locating objects in space, and experiencing one's own body as it moves through space.

29. The _____ lobes of the cortex are involved in movement, attention, planning, social skills, abstract thinking, memory, and some aspects of personality.

30. The _____ lobes of the cortex are particularly important in audition and language.

31. In general, the _____ hemisphere tends to be dominant for language, logic, complex motor behavior, and aspects of consciousness (particularly verbal aspects), whereas the _____ tends to be dominant for nonlinguistic functions.

32. If both alleles are the same, the genotype is called _____, whereas is the two alleles are different, the genotype is called _____.

33. _____ twins develop from the union of the same sperm and egg. Their degree of relatedness is _____.

34. A _____ coefficient quantifies the extent to which variation in a trait across individuals can be accounted for by genetic variation.

35. The term _____ refers to the situation where members of a previously common gene pool have become separated, and over time genetic drift has acted to such an extent that the two subpopulations can no longer interbreed.

36. The process by which people with some discrediting feature are excluded from social interactions is referred to as _____.

APPLICATION

In each of the following hypothetical examples, an individual has suffered an injury to some area of the brain. Try to determine, from what you've read in Chapter 3, where the injury may be.

1.　Following neurosurgery to control life-threatening seizures, a patient is unable to remember new information. You have interviewed this patient on several occasions, yet every time you meet with her, she introduces herself anew to you.

2.　Following a car accident in which her head violently struck the dashboard, a patient reports difficulty focusing attention, motivating herself, and thinking abstractly.

3.　Following a stroke, a patient has difficulty understanding words and sentences spoken by others. She does attempt to speak, and her speech has normal rhythm and fluency; however, it makes little sense – it's a "word salad."

USING WHAT YOU HAVE LEARNED

In Chapter 3, the sympathetic nervous system was described as an emergency system that is activated in response to threats. Its job is to ready the body for fight or flight, and it does so in several ways. Anxiety and panic attacks were described as the result of such sympathetic activity, where the autonomic nervous system may over-react to an event in the environment. Think back to a situation in which you recently experienced anxiety. It may have been a situation where you had to speak before a group of people. Maybe it involved writing an examination. Or maybe it was flying or riding in a fast moving elevator.

1.　What kind of physical sensations did you experience?

2.　Can you see how those sensations reflect the functioning of the sympathetic nervous system?

3.　Can you see the potentially adaptive role those sensations might have, had you been experiencing real physical threat?

4.　Think of the role the adrenal glands play in such a situation. Can you remember feeling aroused and jittery for some time even after the event had passed because of the higher levels of adrenalin in your blood?

PART THREE: TEST AND KNOW
SAMPLE TEST QUESTIONS

Test how well you have learned this chapter's material by answering the sample test questions. You may wish to mark your answers on a separate sheet of paper so you can reuse this test for exam review. Once you have completed the exam, check your answers and then go back to your notes and the textbook to review questions you found difficult.

1.   The nervous system is comprised of three types of neurons:

    a.   sensory neurons, motor neurons, and interneurons
    b.   sensory neurons, spinal neurons, and interneurons
    c.   myelinated axons, dendrites, and unmyelinated axons and dendrites
    d.   sensory neurons, motor neurons, and efferent neurons

2.   The "gray matter" of the brain gets its color from

    a.   myelinated axons
    b.   cell bodies, dendrites, and unmyelinated axons
    c.   synapses
    d.   myelinated cell bodies and dendrites

3.   Connections between neurons occur at what are called

    a.   terminal buttons   b.   nodes of Ranvier
    c.   receptors   d.   synapses

4.   Unlike a graded potential, _____ has an "*all-or-none*" quality.

    a.   an action potential   b.   a resting potential
    c.   depolarization   d.   hyperpolarization

5.   Some people respond to MSG in Chinese food with neurological symptoms such as tingling and numbing, because the ingredient activates _____ receptors in their brains.

    a.   GABA   b.   glutamate
    c.   dopamine   d.   acetylcholine

6.   Parkinson's disease results from degeneration of the _____-releasing cells of the substantia nigra.

    a.   acetylcholine   b.   serotonin
    c.   dopamine   d.   endorphin

7.   The neurotransmitter involved in the regulation of mood, sleep, eating, emotional arousal, and pain regulation is

   a.   dopamine   b.   serotonin
   c.   acetylcholine   d.   endorphin

8.   The endocrine gland(s) that is (are) more directly connected to the CNS than any other endocrine gland is (are) the

   a.   thyroid gland   b.   adrenal glands
   c.   pituitary gland   d.   gonads

9.   The nervous system that prepares the body for fighting or fleeing in response to threats is the

   a.   parasympathetic nervous systemb.   somatic nervous system
   c.   peripheral nervous system   d.   sympathetic nervous system

10.   The area of the hindbrain responsible for maintaining consciousness, regulating arousal levels, and modulating the activity of neurons throughout the central nervous system is the

   a.   medulla oblongata   b.   cerebellum
   c.   reticular activating system   d.   thalamus

11.   One of the most important functions of the hypothalamus is

   a.   relaying sensory information to higher brain centers
   b.   maintaining consciousness and regulating activity states
   c.   homeostasis
   d.   coordinating smooth, well-sequenced movements

12.   The structure within the limbic system that is especially involved in learning and remembering emotionally significant events is the

   a.   amygdala
   b.   hippocampus
   c.   septal area
   d.   basal ganglia

13.   The occipital lobes of the cerebral cortex are involved in

   a.   the sense of touch and the experience of one's own body in space.
   b.   visual sensation and perception.
   c.   attention, planning, abstract thinking, and social skills.
   d.   auditory sensation and perception and language.

14. A brain-injured patient has difficulty putting together grammatical sentences and articulating words, even though he remains able to comprehend language. The area of the brain that is most likely damaged is located in the

   a.   frontal lobes   b.   parietal lobes
   c.   occipital lobes   d.   temporal lobes

15. In most people, the right hemisphere is dominant for

   a.   language   b.   logic
   c.   analytical thinking   d.   recognition of faces and places

16. On the average, males score higher than females on tests of

   a.   manual dexterity   b.   verbal fluency
   c.   perceptual speed   d.   spatial processing

17. Psychologists interested in genetics study the influence of genetic blueprints, referred to as _____, on observable psychological attributes or qualities, referred to as _____.

   a.   chromosomes; genes
   b.   phenotypes; genotypes
   c.   genotypes; phenotypes
   d.   heritability coefficients; degree of relatedness

18. Which type of twins have as much in common, in terms of degree of relatedness, as they have with each of their parents?

   a.   monozygotic twins
   b.   dizygotic twins
   c.   homozygous twins
   d.   heterozygous twins

19. The term "heritability" refers to

   a.   genetic influences on variability among individuals
   b.   the extent to which a trait is genetically determined
   c.   the degree to which various relatives share genetic material
   d.   the degree to which MZ twins and DZ twins differ on a particular trait

20. Chomsky argued that humans are born with what he called a _____ device, an innate set of neural structures for acquiring language.

   a.   syntactical processing   b.   language processing
   c.   grammatical awareness   d.   language acquisition

ANSWERS

FILL-IN EXERCISES

1. sensory (or afferent); motor (or efferent)   2. dendrites; axon   3. white; axons   4. myelin
5. buttons   6. synapses   7. increase   8. action potential   9. neurotransmitters 10. excitatory; inhibitory
11. excite; inhibitory   12. substantia nigra   13. acetylcholine (ACh)   14. epinephrine
15. pituitary   16. thyroid   17. testes, testosterone; ovaries, estrogen 18. psychoneuroimmunology
19. somatic   20. sympathetic   21. spinal cord   22. cerebellum   23. reticular activating   24. thalamus
25. limbic   26. gyri; sulci   27. primary; association 28. parietal   29. frontal   30. temporal   31. left; right
32. homozygous; heterozygous   33. monozygotic; 1.0   34. heritability   35. speciation   36. stigmatization

APPLICATION

1. hippocampus   2. frontal lobes   3. Wernicke's area

SAMPLE TEST QUESTIONS

1.	a	11.	c
2.	b	12.	a
3.	d	13.	b
4.	a	14.	a
5.	b	15.	d
6.	c	16.	d
7.	b	17.	c
8.	c	18.	b
9.	d	19.	a
10.	c	20.	d

Chapter 4
Sensation and Perception

PART ONE: PRE-READ AND WORK
Outline and Learning Objectives

Pre-read this chapter's table of contents and end-of-chapter summary. Then, use the outline segment-by-segment to help you work through the chapter. Jot down your own questions, comments, and notes in the space provided. Make a note of key terms and of difficult areas that you will need to review (include page numbers). Then, answer the questions in the learning objectives section that follows. Check off those you are confident that you can answer well. Re-read the material in the text for the questions about which you are less confident. Record the important points from your reading in the space below each question.

OUTLINE

Basic Principles

Sensing the Environment

Transduction

Absolute Thresholds

One Step Further: Signal Detection

Difference Thresholds

Sensory Adaptation

Vision

The Nature of Light

The Eye

Neural Pathways

Perceiving in Color

Hearing

The Nature of Sound

The Ear

Neural Pathways

Other Senses

Smell

Taste

Skin Senses

From Brain to Behavior: Personality and Pain

Proprioceptive Senses

Perception

Organizing Sensory Experience

A Global Vista: Culture and Perceptual Illusions

Interpreting Sensory Experience

LEARNING OBJECTIVES

Upon completion of Chapter 4, you should be able to answer the following questions.

1.   How does perception differ from sensation?

2.   What three general principles underlie the processes of sensation and perception?

3.   Explain the following five features that are common to all sensory modalities:

Transduction

Absolute thresholds

Signal detection

Difference threshold

Sensory adaptation

4.   What is Weber's law? Fechner's law? Stevens's power law? What are the strengths and weaknesses of each?

5.   Describe the path light travels as it enters the eye and is focused on the retina.

6.   How do photoreceptors transform light into sight?

7.   What are receptive fields and what is their function?

8.   Describe the neural pathway followed by impulses from the optic nerve to the visual cortex.

9.   What is the role of feature detectors in the primary visual cortex? How do simple cells, complex cells, and hypercomplex cells differ from each other?

10.   Differentiate between "what" and "where" pathways.

11.   What is the trichromatic theory of color?

12.   What is the opponent-process theory of color, and how does it explain afterimages and color blindness?

13.   What is the difference between the acoustic energy properties of frequency, complexity, and amplitude?

14.   What are the roles of the outer, middle, and inner ear in the process of hearing?

15.   How do place theory and frequency theory explain the experiences of pitch and loudness?

16.   Describe the neural pathway followed by impulses from the auditory nerve to the auditory cortex.

17.   How do humans localize sound?

18.   How is smell transduced?

19.   Describe the path to the brain followed by information from the smell receptors.

20.   How is taste transduced?

21.   Describe the path to the brain followed by information from the taste receptors.

22.   What is meant by the term *phantom limbs*?

23.   What are the three qualities that constitute the sense of touch?

24.   Are chronic pain and personality style related?

25.   Describe two proprioceptive senses -- kinesthesia and the vestibular sense.

26.   Distinguish among the following four aspects of perceptual organization: form perception, depth perception, motion perception, and perceptual constancy.

27.   What are the six basic perceptual rules, according to Gestalt psychologists, that the brain follows as it organizes sensory input into meaningful wholes?

28.   What is Biederman's *recognition-by-components* theory? How would it explain channel surfing?

29.   How do binocular cues differ from monocular cues? How do these types of cues provide information about depth and distance?

30.   Describe eight monocular depth cues outlined in the text.

31.   What are two systems that appear involved in processing movement?

32.   Explain each of the following forms of perceptual constancy:

Color constancy

Shape constancy

Size constancy

33.   How is size constancy involved in the Müller-Lyer and the Ponzo illusions? In what ways do culture and experience affect susceptibility to these illusions?

34.   Does the visual cliff offer evidence for the phenomenon of direct perception?

35.   Can *bottom-up* and *top-down* processing be viewed as complementary approaches?

36.   How do context and schemas influence the interpretation of experience?

37.   Can motivation influence perception?

PART TWO: REVIEW AND LEARN
Key Terms, Fill-In Exercises, Application and Using What You Have Learned

Before doing the exercises below, review the information you learned in this chapter. Reread the work you did in part one of this study guide chapter, plus the interim summaries and end-of-chapter summary in your textbook. Review any problem areas. Once you feel comfortable with the material, do the following exercises without referring to your notes or textbook. If you have difficulty with a term or question, mark it and come back to it. When you have finished an exercise, go back to your notes and the textbook to find the answers to the questions that gave you difficulty. Finally, check your answers (key terms against the textbook and the rest against the answer key).

KEY TERMS

Sensation _____

_____

Perception _____

_____

Psychophysics _____

_____

Sensory receptors _____

_____

Transduction _____

_____

Absolute threshold _____

_____

Response bias _____

_____

Difference threshold   _____

_____

Just noticeable difference (jnd)   _____

_____

Weber's law   _____

_____

Fechner's law   _____

_____

Stevens's power law   _____

_____

Sensory adaptation   _____

_____

Wavelengths   _____

_____

Cornea _____

_____

Pupil   _____

_____

Iris   _____

_____

Lens   _____

_____

Accommodation _____

_____

Retina _____

_____

Rods _____

_____

Cones _____

_____

Bipolar cells _____

_____

Ganglion cells _____

_____

Optic nerve _____

_____

Fovea _____

_____

Blind spot _____

_____

Receptive field _____

_____

Blindsight _____

_____

Feature detectors _____

_____

"What" pathway _____

_____

"Where" pathway _____

_____

Hue _____

_____

Young-Helmholtz (trichromatic) theory of color _____

_____

Opponent-process theory _____

_____

Audition_____

_____

Sound waves _____

_____

Cycle _____

_____

Frequency _____

_____

Hertz (Hz) _____

_____

Pitch _____

_____

Complexity _____

_____

Timbre _____

_____

Amplitude _____

_____

Decibels (Db) _____

_____

Eardrum (tympanic membrane) _____

_____

Cochlea _____

_____

Hair cells _____

_____

Auditory nerve _____

_____

Place theory _____

_____

Frequency theory _____

_____

Sound localization   _____

_____

Olfaction   _____

_____

Pheromones   _____

_____

Olfactory epithelium   _____

_____

Olfactory nerve _____

_____

Gustation   _____

_____

Taste buds   _____

_____

Phantom limbs _____

_____

Proprioceptive senses_____

_____

Vestibular sense   _____

_____

Kinesthesia   _____

_____

Perceptual organization _____

_____

Form perception_____

_____

Figure-ground perception   _____

_____

Similarity   _____

_____

Proximity   _____

_____

Good continuation   _____

_____

Simplicity   _____

_____

Closure _____

_____

Recognition-by-components   _____

_____

Perceptual illusions   _____

_____

Depth (or distance) perception   _____

_____

Binocular cues _____

_____

Monocular cues _____

_____

Binocular cells _____

_____

Motion parallax _____

_____

Motion perception _____

_____

Motion detectors _____

_____

Perceptual constancy _____

_____

Color constancy _____

_____

Shape constancy _____

_____

Size constancy _____

_____

Müller–Lyer illusion _____

_____

Perceptual interpretation _____

_____

Direct perception   _____

_____

Visual cliff   _____

_____

Bottom-up processing   _____

_____

Top-down processing   _____

_____

Schemas   _____

_____

FILL-IN EXERCISES

Fill in the word or words that best fit in the spaces below.

1.   _____ are immediate experiences of qualities -- such as red, hot, bright, and so forth – whereas _____ are experiences of objects or events that appear to have form, order, or meaning.

2.   _____ is the branch of psychology that studies the relation between attributes of the physical world and our psychological experience of them.

3.   The _____ world – the world as subjectively experienced by an individual -- is a joint product of external reality and the person's creative efforts to understand and depict it mentally.

4.   The process of converting physical energy or stimulus information into neural impulses is referred to as _____.

5.   The minimal amount of physical energy needed for an observer to notice a stimulus is called a(n) _____ _____.

6.   In signal detection tasks, the term _____ _____ refers to the individual's readiness to report detecting a stimulus when he or she is uncertain.

7. The _____ _____ is the lowest level of stimulation required to sense that a change in stimulation has occurred.

8. _____ law states that as the perceived intensity of a stimulus grows arithmetically, the actual magnitude of the stimulus grows exponentially.

9. Sensory _____ refers to the tendency of sensory receptors to respond less to stimuli that continue without change.

10. Light enters the eye through the _____, a tough, transparent tissue covering the front of the eyeball.

11. The retina contains two types of photoreceptors: _____ which respond to color, as well as black and white, and _____ which produce visual sensations in black, white, and gray, only.

12. The central region of the retina, the _____, is most sensitive to small detail, so vision is sharpest for stimuli directly at this spot on the retina. In contrast, the _____ _____, the point on the retina where the ganglion cell axons leave the eye, has no receptor cells.

13. Hubel and Wiesel discovered _____ _____ in the cortex, specialized neurons that fire only when stimulation in their receptive field matches a very specific pattern.

14. The _____ pathway, which runs from the striate cortex in the occipital lobes through the lower part of the temporal lobes, is involved in determining what an object is. The _____ pathway, which runs from the striate cortex through the upper and middle regions of the temporal lobes and up into the parietal lobes, is involved in locating the object in space, following its movement, and guiding movement toward it.

15. The three psychological dimensions of color are _____, _____, and _____.

16. The _____ theory of color holds that the eye contains three types of receptors, each maximally sensitive to wavelengths of light that produce sensations of blue, green, or red.

17. Young adults can hear frequencies from about _____ to about _____ Hertz (Hz), but, as with most senses, capacity diminishes with age.

18. _____ refers to the height and depth of a wave and corresponds to the psychological property of _____.

19. The process of hearing begins in the _____ ear, where sound waves are funneled into the ear by the _____, the skin-covered cartilage that protrudes from the sides of the head.

20. Failure of the outer or middle ear to conduct sound to the receptors in the hair cells is called _____ loss. Failure of receptors in the inner ear or of neurons in any auditory pathway in the brain is referred to as _____ loss.

21.   The _____ is a three-chambered tube in the inner ear shaped like a snail and involved in the transduction of sound.

22.   _____ theory holds that different areas of the basilar membrane are maximally sensitive to different frequencies.

23.   Humans use two main cues for sound localization: differences in between the two ears in _____ and _____ of the sound.

24.   Many species communicate through _____ -- scent messages detected through an auxiliary olfactory system, that regulate the sexual behavior of many animals and direct a variety of behaviors in insects.

25.   Transduction of smell occurs in the _____ _____, a thin pair of structures (one on each side) less than a square inch in diameter at the top of the nasal cavities.

26.   Transduction of taste occurs in the _____ _____, most of which are located on the bumps on the surface of the tongue, called _____.

27.   The gustatory system responds to four basic tastes: _____, _____, _____, and _____.

28.   Sensitivity to pressure varies considerably over the surface of the body. The most sensitive regions are the _____ and _____, and the least sensitive are the _____ and _____.

29.   Of all of the senses, _____ is probably the most affected by beliefs, expectations, and emotional states, and the least reducible to level of stimulation.

30.   Aside from the five traditional senses -- vision, hearing, smell, taste, and touch -- two additional proprioceptive senses, namely _____ and the _____ sense, provide information about the body's position and movement.

31.   _____ _____ refers to the organization of sensations into meaningful shapes and patterns.

32.   The Gestalt principle of _____ refers to the tendency to perceive incomplete figures as complete.

33.   The monocular cue of _____ occurs when one object blocks part of another, leading to perception of the obstructed object as more distant.

34.   When people move, images of nearby objects sweep across their field of vision faster than objects farther away. This disparity in apparent velocity produces a depth cue called _____ _____.

35.   The visual perception of movement begins in the retina itself, with ganglion cells called _____ _____ that are particularly sensitive to movement.

36.   Three types of perceptual constancy are _____ constancy, _____ constancy, and _____ constancy.

37.   Generating meaning from sensory experience is the task of _____ _____.

38.   Whereas Kant emphasized the way the mind orders perception, James Gibson emphasized the way the world organizes perception, so that we detect the order that exists in nature – a theory known as _____ _____.

39.   _____-_____ processing begins with raw sensory data that feed "up" to the brain. In contrast, _____-_____ processing starts with the person's expectations and knowledge, which the brain uses to organize and interpret sensations as soon as the information starts coming in.

40.   Experience with the environment shapes perceptual interpretation by creating perceptual expectations, called _____ _____.

41.   _____ are patterns of thinking about a domain that render the environment relatively predictable.

APPLICATION

Situation

You've been lucky to land a job assisting a cross-cultural psychologist interested in how spatial perception in people from a non-Western culture differs from that of individuals from Western society. She has been conducting research recently with a group of people living in an isolated mountain community with no roads, no television, and little contact with outsiders. Several of them agree to participate in your research. It's exciting to have the opportunity to examine spatial perception from a cross-cultural perspective.

Questions to Answer

1.   How would you expect the three-dimensional perceptual abilities of these participants to compare with those of individuals from your own culture?

2.   These individuals have had no exposure to Western architecture. What influence might this have on their perceptual abilities? Compared with an individual from a city, would you expect them to be more or less susceptible to the *Müller-Lyer* illusion? What about the *Ponzo* illusion? Why?

3.   If, as young children, these individuals had participated in research employing the "visual cliff" apparatus, how would you have expected them to react? According to Gibson's theory of direct perception, how would they react compared to children reared in Western society?

4.   Based on your research, what conclusions would you likely draw regarding the influence of culture and experience on perception?

USING WHAT YOU HAVE LEARNED

Having just studied the topics of sensation and perception, you likely have a great deal of new insight into a number of "real life" questions that puzzle a lot of people. Based on what you have read, address each of the following questions.

1.   When the lights come on in the theater at the end of a movie, why do they seem so much brighter than when you first entered the theater before the movie started?

2.   Does an X-ray of your leg actually look different to a radiologist than to the average person?

3.   When you first walk into a crowded room, why does the noise seem unbearable, but after a few minutes, you hardly even notice it?

4.   Why can your dog hear a "silent" dog whistle, while you can't?

5.   Is grass really green, to a cow?

6.   How are blind people able to read the raised dots that constitute Braille?

7.   Why is it that whenever you have a head-cold and cannot smell because of your stuffy nose, all the food you eat tastes bland?

8.   Why does a needle seem to hurt less when the doctor distracts you by talking or telling a joke?

9.   How is it that you can see colored images on your color television?

10.   Why does your singing sound so much better in the shower than it sounds out of the shower?

PART THREE: TEST AND KNOW
SAMPLE TEST QUESTIONS

Test how well you have learned this chapter's material by answering the sample test questions. You may wish to mark your answers on a separate sheet of paper so you can reuse this test for exam review. Once you have completed the exam, check your answers and then go back to your notes and the textbook to review questions you found difficult.

1.   Which of the following features is *not* shared by all sensory modalities?

   a.   a one-to-one correspondence between physical and psychological reality
   b.   the ability to translate physical stimulation into sensory signals
   c.   the ability to detect changes in stimulation
   d.   a specific threshold -- below which a person does not sense anything, despite external stimulation

2.   Johannes Müller proposed that whether a neural message is experienced as light, sound, or some other sensation results less from differences in stimuli than from the particular neurons excited by them. This hypothesis is known as:

   a.   the Müller–Lyer illusion   b.   Müller's law
   c.   opponent-process theory   d.   the doctrine of specific nerve energies

3.   One type of correct response that may be given by subjects participating in a signal detection experiment is a correct negative. In this event, the subject would report

   a.   a stimulus when an actual stimulus was presented
   b.   a stimulus when no actual stimulus was presented
   c.   no stimulus when no actual stimulus was presented
   d.   no stimulus, when an actual stimulus was presented

4.   Focusing in the eye occurs in the

   a.   iris   b.   retina
   c.   lens   d.   aqueous humor

5.   The central region of the retina, which is most sensitive to small detail and provides sharpest vision for stimuli directly in sight, is the

   a.   vitreous humor   b.   fovea
   c.   rods   d.   optic nerve

6.   Transduction in the eye starts with

   a.   impulses from the optic nerve passing through the optic tracts
   b.   visual information traveling to the primary visual cortex, in the occipital lobes
   c.   neurons in the lateral geniculate nucleus receiving input from the reticular formation
   d.   the focusing of images onto the retina

7.   A neurologist has just shown Samir an object, but Samir denies seeing it. Yet, when asked to describe the geometrical form of the object, Samir is able to do so with accuracy far better than one would expect simply by chance. The neurologist is likely to diagnose Samir as suffering from

   a.   amnesia.   b.   blindsight.
   c.   blindness.   d.   kinesthesia.

8.   Which of the following theories argues that all colors are derived from three antagonistic color systems: a black-white system, a blue-yellow system, and a red-green system?

   a.   place theory   b.   opponent-process theory
   c.   trichromatic theory of color   d.   the doctrine of specific nerve energies

9.   When blue and yellow paints are mixed, green is produced. This is because:

    a.   only the wavelengths not absorbed by *either* the blue or the yellow pigments reach the eye, which is what we perceive as green.
    b.   the wavelengths produced by blue and yellow pigments combine in the retina to give the impression of green.
    c.   the increase in saturation resulting from the combination of these two primary colors gives the impression of green.
    d.   blue, yellow, and red are primary colors according to the *trichromatic theory of color*. All other colors result from the mixing of these primary colors.

10.   People recognize each other's voices, as well as the sounds of different musical instruments, from their characteristic

    a.   frequency   b.   pitch
    c.   timbre   d.   amplitude

11.   The outer boundary of the middle ear is marked by the _____.

    a.   eustachian tube   b.   cochlea
    c.   malleus   d.   tympanic membrane

12.   In terms of sensing pitch, *place theory* holds that

    a.   different areas of the basilar membrane are maximally sensitive to different frequencies
    b.   the more frequently a sound wave cycles, the more frequently the basilar membrane vibrates and hair cells fire
    c.   the place where an observer stands while looking at an object can result in an auditory feeling of depth perception
    d.   the location or place from which a sound originates can be identified by means of sound localization

13.   Gustatory information travels to one of two destinations in the brain: one via the thalamus to the primary gustatory cortex, and the other to the limbic system. People with damage to the first (cortical) pathway, but not to the second

    a.   fail to identify substances by taste, but react with appropriate affective and behavioral responses to tastes
    b.   can identify substances by taste, but fail to show appropriate affective or behavioral response to tastes
    c.   cannot identify substances by taste and fail to react with the appropriate affective and behavioral responses to tastes
    d.   can identify substances by taste and show an immediate affective or behavioral response to tastes

14. The approximately _____ square feet of skin covering the human body constitutes a complex, multilayered organ.

   a.   2   b.   10
   c.   18   d.   25

15. People spend billions of dollars a year fighting pain, but pain serves an important function in that

   a.   it builds character
   b.   it prevents tissue damage
   c.   it indicates the presence of the disorder "painful neuropathy"
   d.   it distracts us from the worries of modern life

16. Researchers have identified a personality style that appears to be shared by many chronic pain patients. These patients tend to

   a.   blame their physical condition for all life's difficulties, while denying emotional and interpersonal problems
   b.   be anxious, needy, and dependent
   c.   have difficulty expressing anger
   d.   all of the above

17. The two organs that transduce vestibular information are called _____, and are located _____.

   a.   the semicircular canals and the vestibular sacs; in the inner ear
   b.   the tendons and the muscles; in the joints
   c.   the pinna and the tympanic membrane; in the outer ear
   d.   kinesthesia and the vestibular sense; in the medulla

18. Which of the following is *not* a perceptual rule by which the brain automatically and unconsciously organizes sensory input into meaningful wholes, according to Gestalt psychologists?

   a.   proximity   b.   shading
   c.   good continuation   d.   simplicity

19. Generating meaning from sensory experience is the task of

   a.   perceptual organization   b.   direct perception
   c.   perceptual constancy   d.   perceptual interpretation

20. According to current thinking, perception involves

   a.   top-down processing   b.   bottom-up processing
   c.   both of the above   d.   neither of the above

ANSWERS

FILL-IN EXERCISES

1. sensations; perceptions 2. psychophysics 3. phenomenological   4. transduction 5. absolute threshold
6. response bias   7. difference threshold 8. Stevens's power 9. adaptation 10. cornea 11. cones; rods
12. fovea; blind spot (optic disk)   13. feature detectors   14. what; where   15. hue, saturation, lightness
16. Young-Helmholtz (or trichromatic)   17. 15; 20,000   18. amplitude; loudness   19. outer; pinna
20. conduction; sensorineural   21. cochlea 22. place 23. loudness; timing   24. pheromones
25. olfactory epithelium   26. taste buds; papillae 27. sweet, sour, salty, bitter   28. face, fingers; back, legs
29. pain 30. kinesthesia; vestibular 31. form perception   32. closure 33. interposition
34. motion parallax 35. motion detectors   36. color; shape; size   37. perceptual interpretation
38. direct perception 39. bottom-up; top-down 40. perceptual set   41. schemas

APPLICATION

1. Their experience with binocular and many monocular cues would provide information about depth. Their depth perception should, therefore, be as good as that of anyone else.

2. Lack of roads joining at angles, rectangular buildings, and so on would result in less experience with the cues that give rise to Müller-Lyer illusion. Lack of experience with lines converging in the distance (e.g., roads, railway tracks) would lead to less susceptibility to Ponzo illusion.

3. As they began to crawl, they would have been reluctant to cross to the deep side of the cliff. According to Gibson's theory, both the understanding of depth cues and the meaning of falling off the cliff may be inborn in humans.

4. Early experience shapes the neural systems underlying sensation and perception. Some perceptual abilities are influenced by culture-specific experiences (e.g., architecture and angles); others seem uninfluenced by culture (e.g., avoidance of deep side on visual cliff) and may even be innate.

SAMPLE TEST QUESTIONS

1.	a	11.	d
2.	d	12.	a
3.	c	13.	a
4.	c	14.	c
5.	b	15.	b
6.	d	16.	d
7.	b	17.	a
8.	b	18.	b
9.	a	19.	d
10.	c	20.	c

Chapter 5
Learning

PART ONE: PRE-READ AND WORK
Outline and Learning Objectives

Pre-read this chapter's table of contents and end-of-chapter summary. Then, use the outline segment-by-segment to help you work through the chapter. Jot down your own questions, comments, and notes in the space provided. Make a note of key terms and of difficult areas that you will need to review (include page numbers). Then, answer the questions in the learning objectives section that follows. Check off those you are confident that you can answer well. Re-read the material in the text for the questions about which you are less confident. Record the important points from your reading in the space below each question.

OUTLINE

Classical Conditioning

Pavlov's Model

Conditioned Responses

Stimulus Generalization and Discrimination

Extinction

Factors That Affect Classical Conditioning

What Do Organisms Learn in Classical Conditioning?

From Brain to Behavior: The Neural Basis of Classical Conditioning

Operant Conditioning

Reinforcement

Punishment

Extinction

Operant Conditioning of Complex Behaviors

One Step Further: Why Are Reinforcers Reinforcing?

Cognitive-Social Theory

Learning and Cognition

A Global Vista: Optimism, Pessimism, and Expectancies of Control in Cross-Cultural Perspective

Social Learning

LEARNING OBJECTIVES

Upon completion of Chapter 5, you should be able to answer the following questions.

1.   What are the three assumptions shared by theories of learning?

2.   What are the basic principles underlying Pavlov's model of conditioning?

3.   What are the differences between an unconditioned stimulus (UCS) and a conditioned stimulus (CS), and between an unconditioned response (UCR) and a conditioned response (CR)?

4.   What are conditioned taste aversions and how can they be explained in terms of classical conditioning?

5.   How did John Watson produce a conditioned emotional response in little Albert?

6.   Can the functioning of the immune system be affected by classical conditioning?

7.   How does stimulus generalization differ from stimulus discrimination?

8.   What is involved in the processes of extinction and spontaneous recovery?

9.   How does the time between the presentation of the CS and UCS influence conditioning?

10.   Describe the temporal order of the CS and UCS in each of the following:

Forward conditioning

Simultaneous conditioning

Backward conditioning

11.   In what ways can *blocking* and *latent inhibition* interfere with learning?

12.   What are the shortcomings of Aristotle's *law of contiguity*? How does Rescorla and Wagner's *law of prediction* better explain what is learned in classical conditioning?

13.   What is the phenomenon of *paradoxical conditioning*?

14.   Discuss the notion that animals may be biologically prepared to learn some associations more easily than others.

15.   Explain how research suggests that learning occurs through changes in the strength of connections between neurons.

16.   How does operant conditioning differ from classical conditioning?

17.   How does reinforcement differ from punishment? Provide illustrations of positive and negative reinforcement, as well as positive and negative punishment.

18.   How does operant learning theory explain superstitious behavior?

19.   What are five common drawbacks associated with the use of punishment?

20.   How does partial reinforcement differ from continuous reinforcement? Describe four types of partial reinforcement schedules and their effects on responding.

21.   Provide several everyday examples of discriminative stimuli signaling the occurrence of particular contingencies of reinforcement.

22.   Explain what is meant by the term *behavioral economics*.

23.   How can shaping and chaining be used to teach complex behaviors?

24.   How does drive reduction account for the reinforcing value of certain stimuli?

25.   How do secondary reinforcers acquire their reinforcing properties?

26.   What are the roles of the behavioral approach system (BAS) the behavioral inhibition system (BIS), and the fight-flight system in the learning of operant behavior?

27.   Does the phenomenon of latent learning provide evidence for the role of cognition in learning?

28.   Do animals other than humans have the capacity for insight?

29.   What is meant by the term locus of control? How do people with an internal locus of control differ from those with an external locus of control?

30.   In what ways do individuals with a pessimistic explanatory style interpret negative events in a depressive manner?

21.   Discuss how each of the following play a role in social learning:

Modeling

Vicarious conditioning

Tutelage

PART TWO: REVIEW AND LEARN
Key Terms, Fill-In Exercises, Application and Using What You Have Learned

Before doing the exercises below, review the information you learned in this chapter. Reread the work you did in part one of this study guide chapter, plus the interim summaries and end-of-chapter summary in your textbook. Review any problem areas. Once you feel comfortable with the material, do the following exercises without referring to your notes or textbook. If you have difficulty with a term or question, mark it and come back to it. When you have finished an exercise, go back to your notes and the textbook to find the answers to the questions that gave you difficulty. Finally, check your answers (key terms against the textbook and the rest against the answer key).

KEY TERMS

Learning _____

_____

Reflex _____

_____

Stimulus _____

_____

Habituation _____

_____

Laws of association _____

_____

Classical conditioning _____

_____

Conditioning _____

_____

Unconditioned stimulus (UCS) _____

_____

Unconditioned response (UCR) _____

_____

Conditioned response (CR) _____

_____

Conditioned stimulus (CS) _____

_____

Phobias _____

_____

Immune system _____

_____

Stimulus generalization _____

_____

Galvanic skin response (GSR) _____

_____

Stimulus discrimination _____

_____

Extinction _____

_____

Spontaneous recovery _____

_____

Interstimulus interval _____

_____

Blocking _____

_____

Latent inhibition _____

_____

Prepared learning _____

_____

Long-term potentiation (LTP) _____

_____

Law of effect _____

_____

Operant conditioning _____

_____

Operants _____

_____

Reinforcement _____

_____

Punishment _____

_____

Reinforcer _____

_____

Positive reinforcement _____

_____

Positive reinforcer _____

_____

Superstitious behavior _____

_____

Negative reinforcement _____

_____

Negative reinforcer _____

_____

Escape learning _____

_____

Avoidance learning _____

_____

Continuous reinforcement schedule _____

_____

Partial or intermittent schedule of reinforcement _____

_____

Ratio schedules _____

_____

Interval schedules _____

_____

Fixed ratio (FR) schedule

_____

_____

Variable ratio (VR) schedule

_____

_____

Fixed interval (FI) schedule

_____

_____

Variable interval (VI) schedule

_____

_____

Discriminative stimulus (S^D)

_____

_____

Shaping

_____

_____

Biofeedback

_____

_____

Chaining

_____

_____

Drive

_____

_____

Drive-reduction theory

_____

_____

Primary reinforcers

_____

_____

Secondary reinforcers _____

_____

Behavioral approach system (BAS)   _____

_____

Behavioral inhibition system (BIS)   _____

_____

Fight-flight system   _____

_____

Cognitive-social theory _____

_____

Cognitive maps _____

_____

Latent learning _____

_____

Insight _____

_____

Expectancies   _____

_____

Self-fulfilling prophecy   _____

_____

Generalized expectancies   _____

_____

Locus of control of reinforcement_____

_____

Internal locus of control _____

_____

External locus of control _____

_____

Learned helplessness _____

_____

Explanatory style _____

_____

Pessimistic explanatory style _____

_____

Social learning _____

_____

Observational learning _____

_____

Modeling _____

_____

Vicarious conditioning _____

_____

Tutelage _____

_____

FILL-IN EXERCISES

Fill in the word or words that best fit in the spaces below.

1.   A _____ is a behavior that is elicited automatically by an environmental stimulus.

2.   _____ refers to the decreasing strength of a response after repeated presentations of the stimulus.

3.   Aristotle proposed a set of laws of association to account for learning and memory. The most important was the law of _____, which proposes that two events will become connected in the mind if they are experienced close together in time. Another was the law of _____, which states that objects that resemble each other are likely to become associated.

4.   Classical conditioning involves associating a neutral stimulus with the _____ stimulus. Following several trials, the neutral stimulus will come to elicit the response, and is now referred to as the _____ stimulus.

5.   The fear response that little Albert displayed to the white rat in Watson and Rayner's study is an example of a _____ _____ response.

6.   Many psychologists have proposed classical conditioning as an explanation for human _____, that is, irrational fears of specific objects or situations.

7.   Little Albert's fear of other stimuli that shared certain characteristics with the rat (i.e., furry or hairy objects) is a good example of the phenomenon of _____ _____.

8.   Galvanic skin response (GSR) is an electrical measure of the amount of sweat on the skin and can be used to assess _____.

9.   Stimulus _____ is the learned tendency to respond to a restricted range of stimuli or only to the stimulus used during training.

10.   Each pairing of the CS and UCS is know as a conditioning _____.

11.   Presentation of the CS without the UCS will lead to _____ of the CR.

12.   The duration of time between presentation of the CS and UCS is referred to as the _____ _____.

13.   In classical conditioning, _____ conditioning involves presenting the CS and terminating it before the UCS is presented.

14.   The failure of a stimulus to elicit a conditioned response when it is combined with another stimulus that already elicits the response is called _____.

15.   If a bell repeatedly sounds without presentation of meat, a dog may be slower to learn the connection after the bell *does* start to signal mealtime. This phenomenon is referred to as latent _____.

16.   Fear of snakes and spiders in humans may involve the learning of associations that are biologically _____.

17.   Long-term _____ refers to the tendency of a group of neurons to fire more readily after consistent stimulation from other neurons.

18.   Thorndike's law of _____ states that an animal's tendency to reproduce a behavior depends on that behavior's effect on the environment and the consequent effect on the animal.

19.   Operants are behaviors that are _____ by the organism rather than _____ by the environment.

20.   Negative reinforcement _____ (*increases/decreases*) the probability that a response will occur.

21.   In _____ learning, a behavior is reinforced by the elimination of an aversive state of affairs that already exists, whereas in _____ learning an organism learns to prevent an expected aversive event from happening.

22.   In _____ punishment, exposure to an aversive event following a behavior reduces the likelihood of the behavior recurring. On the other hand, _____ punishment involves losing or not obtaining a reinforcer as a consequence of behavior.

23.   The health inspector checks out each restaurant in town about once per year, but arrives unannounced and unexpectedly. This is an example of a _____ _____ schedule of reinforcement.

24.   A stimulus that signals the presence of particular contingencies of reinforcement is called a _____ stimulus.

25.   _____ produces novel behavior by reinforcing closer and closer approximations to the desired response.

26.   Psychologists use _____ to help patients to gain control over autonomic responses such as heart rate, body temperature, and blood pressure by feeding them information about these responses.

27.   _____ involves putting together a sequence of existing responses into a novel order.

28.   A _____ is a state that impels the organism to act.

29.   A _____ reinforcer is a stimulus that innately reinforces behavior without any prior learning.

30. The behavioral _____ system is associated with anxiety and is involved in negative reinforcement and punishment.

31. Individuals with an _____ locus of control believe that their lives are determined by forces outside themselves.

32. _____ _____ refers to the expectancy that one cannot escape aversive events, which leads to motivational and learning deficits.

33. Observational learning in which a person learns to reproduce behavior exhibited by someone else is called _____.

34. In _____ conditioning, a person learns the consequences of an action by observing its consequences for someone else.

USING WHAT YOU HAVE LEARNED

One of the most difficult problems parents face is when their children display temper tantrums. Kids will scream, roll around on the floor, bang their hands and heads on the floor, hold their breath, and so on until they get what they want. Parents are often embarrassed or concerned that their child might hurt himself or herself. So they often "give in" and let the child have what he or she wanted in order to end the tantrum.

1. In terms of reinforcement, what do you suppose happens when parents give in to the tantrum? How will this likely affect the probability of future tantrums?

2. If giving in stops the tantrum (an aversive stimulus), what are parents likely to do the next time the child throws a tantrum? Why?

3. Often, children learn that there are certain places where parents will give in quickly, such as on the bus or in a quiet place like a library. Kids are all the more likely to throw a tantrum in these places. What do these situations signal to the child? What would be the behavioral term to apply to these situations?

4. What would you advise parents to do to stop the tantrums, based on your understanding of the principles of learning?

APPLICATION

Situation

After his class attended a special kids' performance of the symphony, 8-year-old Billy had been begging his parents to buy him a violin. Finally, they gave in and got him one. The only problem is that he doesn't practice. His teacher says he should practice for half an hour each day, but Billy never does more than 5 minutes. His mom keeps nagging him to practice, but it doesn't work. He practices for 5 minutes, and then he's off to his friend's house. His mom is getting frustrated and is considering canceling his lessons. Having just studied learning in her psychology course, she decides to try applying operant learning principles to change Billy's behavior. She buys an X-Box, to use to reward Billy for practicing for half an hour each day. She realizes, however, that half an hour of practice will initially seem like an eternity to him, and he'll probably give up after only 10 minutes. So, she gets her kitchen timer and tells Billy: "I want you to practice your violin until the bell on the timer rings. When it rings, come and get me and we'll play video games together." The first day, she sets the timer for 5 minutes. The next day, she sets it for 10 minutes. The next day she sets it for 15 minutes, and so on. By the end of the week, Billy is practicing for half an hour.

Questions to Answer

1. In the above situation, playing video games with mom serves as what?

2. Rewarding Billy for practicing his violin for a progressively longer time is an example of what?

3. The bell on the timer serves as what kind of stimulus?

After a couple of weeks, Billy's mom is pleased that he is practicing for half an hour a day, but is finding that she hasn't got the time to play video games with him every day. Yet, when she told him she hasn't got time to play video games any more, Billy's practicing time dropped back to 5 minutes.

4. Billy's drop in practice time after his mom stopped playing video games with him is an example of what principle of learning?

5. In terms of operant learning theory, how could Billy's mom cut back on playing video games, but still keep Billy regularly practicing for half an hour?

PART THREE: TEST AND KNOW
SAMPLE TEST QUESTIONS

Test how well you have learned this chapter's material by answering the sample test questions. You may
wish to mark your answers on a separate sheet of paper so you can reuse this test for exam review. Once
you have completed the exam, check your answers and then go back to your notes and the textbook to
review questions you found difficult.

1.   Many people display severe negative emotional reactions to hypodermic needles, through
        exposure to injections in childhood. These reactions can be explained in terms of:

        a.   instrumental conditioning
        b.   classical conditioning
        c.   blocking
        d.   preparedness to learn

2.   Suppose Watson and Rayner had exposed little Albert repeatedly (i.e., on the second, third, and all
        subsequent trials) to the white rat but without the noise.

        a.   Albert's fear response would have become even stronger.
        b.   Albert's fear response would have generalized to whatever white, furry objects were
                present in the environment.
        c.   Albert's fear response would have extinguished.
        d.   Albert's fear response would have spontaneously recovered.

3.   In classical conditioning, the *least* effective type of conditioning is

        a.   backward conditioning
        b.   forward conditioning
        c.   simultaneous conditioning
        d.   instrumental conditioning

4.   The sight of drug paraphernalia can activate physiological reactions that reduce the effect of the
        heroin an addict is about to take. This likely involves

        a.   stimulus substitution   b.   escape learning
        c.   vicarious conditioning   d.   paradoxical conditioning

5.   Praise is a good example of a(n)

        a.   conditioned stimulus
        b.   unconditioned stimulus
        c.   secondary reinforcer
        d.   vicarious reinforcer

6.   Slot machines are popular in casinos because all you have to do to play is pull the lever. Every so often, after an unpredictable number of pulls, somebody will "hit the jackpot." What schedule of reinforcement is likely in effect here?

    a.   fixed interval   b.   fixed ratio
    c.   variable interval   d.   variable ratio

7.   The fact that people will put money into slot machines and pull the level over and over, especially after seeing someone else hit the jackpot, even though they may have never won anything themselves can be explained in terms of

    a.   avoidance learning
    b.   vicarious conditioning
    c.   classical conditioning
    d.   operant conditioning

8.   Keeping your driving speed below the speed limit so you don't get caught in a radar trap is an example of

    a.   avoidance learning
    b.   escape learning
    c.   shaping
    d.   positive punishment

9.   Removing a child's TV privileges is an example of

    a.   negative reinforcement
    b.   negative punishment
    c.   positive punishment
    d.   secondary reinforcement

10.   Punishment tends to be most effective

    a.   when it is severe
    b.   when it occurs some time after the behavior
    c.   when it is accompanied by reasoning
    d.   punishment is *never* effective

11.   Fishing involves behavior that is difficult to extinguish. People who like fishing will spend hours "on the lake" without catching anything, before finally giving up in frustration. This is because fishing likely involves

    a.   a conditioned emotional response   b.   simultaneous conditioning
    c.   intermittent reinforcement   d.   behavioral economics

12.   The students in Mr. Bebby's grade 8 class have learned not to fool around when he's mad, because he's likely to give the whole class detention. The easiest way to tell when he's mad is that you can see a vein on the side of his forehead begin throbbing. When that vein starts throbbing, the students immediately settle down. Mr. Bebby's throbbing vein is a

    a.   secondary reinforcer
    b.   conditioned stimulus
    c.   conditioned response
    d.   discriminative stimulus

13.   In the above example, settling down when Mr. Bebby's vein starts throbbing is an example of

    a.   superstitious behavior
    b.   a conditioned response
    c.   avoidance learning
    d.   latent learning

14.   Learning to drive a car with a manual transmission involves acquiring a variety of behaviors, such as shifting the gears, using the clutch, using the accelerator, and so on. Putting these together to drive the car smoothly involves

    a.   chaining
    b.   escape learning
    c.   shaping
    d.   simultaneous conditioning

15.   Gray argues that anatomically distinct pathways in the nervous system control different forms of learning and are associated with different emotional states. The system involved in negative reinforcement and punishment is

    a.   the behavioral approach system
    b.   the behavioral inhibition system
    c.   the fight-flight system
    d.   the latent inhibition system

16.   Tolman suggested that rats may form _____ , or mental representations of a maze, even without any reinforcement.

    a.   cognitive maps
    b.   generalized expectancies
    c.   outcome expectancies
    d.   insights

17.   Learning that has occurred, but is not currently manifest in behavior, was described by Tolman as

        a.   latent learning
        b.   discriminative learning
        c.   vicarious learning
        d.   latent inhibition

18.   Everything has been going wrong for Ted. No matter what he tries, it doesn't seem to make any difference. So, he's just given up trying. Ted's behavior is an example of

        a.   avoidance learning
        b.   paradoxical conditioning
        c.   stimulus generalization
        d.   learned helplessness

19.   All of the following *except* one are ways in which individuals with a pessimistic explanatory style see the causes of negative events. Which does not apply?

        a.   internal
        b.   stable
        c.   global
        d.   temporary

20.   After seeing a child get bitten by a dog, little Mario displays an intense fear reaction when he sees a puppy at the pet store. His response can be explained with reference to

        a.   classical conditioning
        b.   vicarious conditioning
        c.   instrumental conditioning
        d.   negative reinforcement

ANSWERS

FILL-IN EXERCISES

1. reflex 2. habituation 3. contiguity; similarity 4. unconditioned; conditioned 5. conditioned emotional 6. phobias 7. stimulus generalization 8. arousal (or anxiety) 9. discrimination 10. trial 11. extinction 12. interstimulus interval 13. forward 14. blocking 15. inhibition 16. prepared 17. potentiation 18. effect 19. emitted; elicited 20. increases 21. escape; avoidance 22. positive; negative 23. variable interval 24. discriminative 25. shaping 26. biofeedback 27. chaining 28. drive 29. primary 30. inhibition 31. external 32. learned helplessness 33. modeling 34. vicarious

USING WHAT YOU HAVE LEARNED

1. The tantrum is positively reinforced, which increases the probability of future tantrums.
2. Parents are more likely to give in the next time the child has a tantrum because stopping the tantrum ends the aversive stimulus and thereby negatively reinforces giving in.
3. These situations signal the presence of particular contingencies of reinforcement (i.e., parents are more likely to give in in these settings). The behavioral term is discriminative stimuli.
4. The behavior should be extinguished – i.e., remove the reinforcing consequences of giving in.

APPLICATION

1. A positive reinforcer
2. Shaping
3. A discriminative stimulus
4. Extinction
5. Partial reinforcement (variable ratio schedule)

SAMPLE TEST QUESTIONS

1.	b	11.	c
2.	c	12.	d
3.	a	13.	c
4.	d	14.	a
5.	c	15.	b
6.	d	16.	a
7.	b	17.	a
8.	a	18.	d
9.	b	19.	d
10.	c	20.	b

Chapter 6
Memory

PART ONE: PRE-READ AND WORK
Outline and Learning Objectives

Pre-read this chapter's table of contents and end-of-chapter summary. Then, use the outline segment-by-segment to help you work through the chapter. Jot down your own questions, comments, and notes in the space provided. Make a note of difficult areas that you will need to review (include page numbers). Then, answer the questions in the learning objectives section that follows. Check off those you are confident that you can answer well. Re-read the material in the text for the questions about which you are less confident. Record the important points from your reading in the space below each question.

OUTLINE

Memory and Information Processing

Mental Representations

Information Processing: An Evolving Model

Working Memory

Processing Information in Working Memory: The Central Executive

Visual and Verbal Storage

One Step Further: The Neuropsychology of Working Memory

The Relation Between Working Memory and Long-Term Memory

Varieties of Long-Term Memory

Declarative and Procedural Memory

Explicit and Implicit Memory

From Brain to Behavior: The Neuropsychology of Long-Term Memory

Everyday Memory

Encoding and Organization of Long-Term Memory

Encoding

Mnemonic Devices

Networks of Association

Schemas

A Global Vista: Cross-Cultural Variation in Memory – Better, Worse, or Just Different?

Remembering, Misremembering, and Forgetting

How Long is Long-Term Memory?

How Accurate is Long-Term Memory?

From Brain to Behavior: Arousal and Memory

Why do People Forget?

Commentary: Repressed Memories of Sexual Abuse

LEARNING OBJECTIVES

Upon completion of Chapter 6, you should be able to answer the following questions.

1.   In what ways do sensory representations differ from verbal representations?

2.   How does iconic storage differ from echoic storage?

3.   What are the major differences between long-term and short-term memory?

4.   How does serial position affect free recall?

5.   What are four major ways in which thinking about memory has evolved over the past decade?

6.   Discuss the storage and processing functions of working memory.

7.   What evidence does neurological research provide for the notion of working memory?

8.   How are working memory and long-term memory related?

9.   What are the differences between declarative and procedural memory?

10.   How are semantic and episodic memory related?

11.   How does explicit memory differ from implicit memory?

12.   Does neurological research support the distinction between explicit and implicit memory?

13.   What has recent research revealed about everyday memory?

14.   How is the accessibility of information in long-term memory influenced by the following:

Level of processing

Spacing

Representational modes

15.   What are two common mnemonic devices?

16.   Explain how pieces of information stored in memory form networks of association.

17.   In what ways is hierarchical organization of information analogous to a filing system?

18.   How are both encoding and retrieval of information affected by schemas?

19.   Can the organization of information in memory be influenced by culture?

20.   What are the "seven sins of memory" described by Daniel Schacter?

21.   Why are some researchers concerned about the accuracy of eyewitness testimony in the courtroom?

22.   What has research shown concerning emotional arousal and flashbulb memories?

23.   What are the differences between the following three explanations of forgetting: decay, interference, and motivated forgetting?

24.   Why is it difficult to scientifically address the issue of false memories of childhood trauma?

PART TWO: REVIEW AND LEARN
Key Terms, Fill-In Exercises, Application and Using What You Have Learned

Before doing the exercises below, review the information you learned in this chapter. Reread the work you did in part one of this study guide chapter, plus the interim summaries and end-of-chapter summary in your textbook. Review any problem areas. Once you feel comfortable with the material, do the following exercises without referring to your notes or textbook. If you have difficulty with a term or question, mark it and come back to it. When you have finished an exercise, go back to your notes and the textbook to find the answers to the questions that gave you difficulty. Finally, check your answers (key terms against the textbook and the rest against the answer key).

KEY TERMS

Upon completion of Chapter 6, you should be able to define the following terms.

Sensory representations _____

_____

Verbal representations _____

_____

Sensory registers   _____

_____

Iconic storage _____

_____

Echoic storage _____

_____

Short-term memory (STM) _____

_____

Rehearsal _____

_____

Maintenance rehearsal _____

_____

Elaborative rehearsal _____

_____

Long-term memory (LTM) _____

_____

Retrieval _____

_____

Serial position effect _____

_____

Modules _____

_____

Working memory _____

_____

Chunking _____

_____

Declarative memory _____

_____

Procedural memory _____

_____

Semantic memory _____

_____

Generic memory _____

_____

Episodic memory _____

_____

Explicit memory _____

_____

Implicit memory _____

_____

Recall _____

_____

Tip-of-the-tongue phenomenon _____

_____

Recognition _____

_____

Priming effects _____

_____

Everyday memory _____

_____

Retrospective memory _____

_____

Prospective memory _____

_____

Encoding _____

_____

Level of processing _____

_____

Encoding specificity principle _____

_____

Retrieval cues _____

_____

Spacing effect _____

_____

Mnemonic devices _____

_____

Method of loci _____

_____

SQ3R method _____

_____

Networks of association _____

_____

Node _____

_____

Spreading activation theory _____

_____

Cultural models _____

_____

Forgetting _____

_____

Flashbulb memories _____

_____

Decay theory _____

_____

Interference _____

_____

Proactive interference _____

_____

Retroactive interference _____

_____

Motivated forgetting   _____

_____

FILL-IN EXERCISES

Fill in the word or words that best fit in the spaces below.

1.   People maintain a mental image (icon) of what they have seen that lasts for approximately _____ to _____ seconds.

2.   The auditory counterpart of iconic storage is _____ storage.

3.   To assess _____-_____ memory, psychologists often measure subjects' digit span; that is, how many numbers they can hold in memory at once.

4.   Short-term memory holds information in consciousness for approximately _____ to _____ seconds, unless the person makes a deliberate attempt to retain it longer by repeating it over and over.

5.   On the average, people can hold about _____ pieces of information in STM, with the normal range from _____ to _____ items.

6.   Mental repetition in order to maintain information in STM is called _____ rehearsal. A procedure that is more useful for storing information in long-term memory is _____ rehearsal, which involves actively thinking about the information while rehearsing.

7.   Recovering information from LTM, known as _____, involves bringing it back into STM.

8.   The tendency for subjects to remember words at the beginning and end of a list better than words that appear in the middle is known as the _____ _____effect.

9.   Researchers have come to view memory as involving a set of _____ -- discrete but interdependent processing units responsible for different kinds of remembering.

10.   Information remains in _____ memory only so long as the person is consciously processing, examining, or manipulating it.

11.   According to one prominent model, working memory consists of three memory systems: a _____ memory store, a _____ memory store, and a _____ _____ that controls and manipulates the information that these two short-term stores hold in mind.

12.   Working memory appears to be orchestrated, or directed, by the _____ _____, a region of the brain long known to be involved in the most high-level cognitive functions.

13.   _____ is a memory technique that uses knowledge stored in LTM to group information in larger units than single words or digits and hence to expand working memory capacity.

14.   Memory for facts and events, much of which can be consciously stated, is referred to as _____ memory.

15.   Semantic memory is also referred to as _____ memory by many psychologists, because such general knowledge is stored in more than just words.

16.   _____ memory consists of memories of particular events, rather than general knowledge.

17.   Memory that is expressed in behavior but does not require conscious recollection is referred to as _____ memory.

18.   Neurological research indicates that the neural structure known as the _____ is central to the consolidation of explicit memories.

19.   _____ memory has at least two components: remembering *to* remember (or *intent*) and remembering *what* to remember (or *content*).

20.   The degree to which information is elaborated, reflected upon, and processed in a meaningful way during memory storage is referred to as _____ of processing

21.   According to the _____ _____ principle, ease of retrieval depends on the match between the way information is encoded and later retrieved.

22.   _____ devices are strategies that people use as memory aids. One such device is the method of _____, which uses visual imagery as a memory aid.

23.   Networks of association involve complex interconnections among _____.

24.   The filing cabinet metaphor suggests that information in LTM tends to be filed _____; that is, broad categories are composed of narrower subcategories, which in turn consist of even more specific categories.

25.   _____ are patterns of thought, or organized knowledge structures that render the environment relatively predictable. They can, however, lead people to misclassify information, to believe they have seen what they really haven't, and to fail to notice things that might be important.

26.   _____ _____ are memories of exciting or highly consequential events.

27.   _____ theory explains forgetting as a result of a fading memory trace.

28.   _____ interference refers to the interference of previous stored memories with the retrieval of new information.

USING WHAT YOU HAVE LEARNED

A group of university students listened to a news report describing how an airline pilot courageously landed a plane safely after its landing gear had failed.

After hearing this story, most of the students described the aircraft as a jet, although there was no mention in the story of what type of aircraft it was. In addition, several of them added details that were not in the news report, such as describing the pilot as male, or adding the observation that it had been raining at the time of the landing.

What type of memory do these phenomena involve? What is likely responsible for the addition of new information about the type of aircraft, the sex of the pilot, and the weather conditions? Have you ever noticed similar errors in your own recall of specific details of events? Could there be any advantage to such aspects of memory?

APPLICATION

Situation

A friend of yours, knowing that you are studying psychology and that you have just finished learning about memory, asks for your advice in how to prepare for an upcoming exam. In terms of what you have covered in this chapter, how would you answer her questions?

1. "When I get into the exam I always just go blank. Are there any 'memory tricks' that will help me remember the important concepts I have to remember?"

2. "I find it best to stay up all night and cram the night before. The only problem is that some of this material will also be on the final next month. Is there a better way to study so that I'll remember more for the final?"

3. "Is it best just to read my notes over and over, or is there some other thing I could be doing?"

4. "Someone told me that it's better to study the material in a different order every time I go over it. You know, tomorrow begin with the material I studied in the middle tonight and end with the beginning material. Next night, begin with the end material. Is there any truth to that? Why would that help?"

5. "Sometimes I find that studying for Italian actually makes it harder to remember the material I previously studied for my French exam. Am I just fooling myself, or could this really happen?"

PART THREE: TEST AND KNOW
SAMPLE TEST QUESTIONS

Test how well you have learned this chapter's material by answering the sample test questions. You may wish to mark your answers on a separate sheet of paper so you can reuse this test for exam review. Once you have completed the exam, check your answers and then go back to your notes and the textbook to review questions you found difficult.

1.   Repeating information over and over again to prevent it from fading is a procedure known as

   a.   echoic storage   b.   priming
   c.   rehearsal   d.   SQ3R method

2.   When a list of words is presented to subjects, they tend to remember those at the beginning and at the end of the list more easily than those in the middle, because of

   a.   the primacy effect   b.   the serial position effect
   c.   the priming process   d.   distributed practice effects

3.   Baddeley and Hitch had subjects perform two tasks simultaneously: one involved recalling a series of digits and the other involved some kind of thinking, such as reasoning or comprehending the meaning of sentences. Their results suggested that

   a.   storage capacity and processing capacity are two separate aspects of working memory
   b.   storage capacity and processing capacity are ultimately the same thing; they are highly interdependent
   c.   short-term memory is too limited to involve working on two tasks simultaneously
   d.   while storage capacity in STM is unlimited, processing capacity is limited to a small number of tasks

4.   Working memory appears to be "orchestrated" by the _____, a region of the brain long known to be involved in most high-level cognitive functions.

   a.   hippocampus   b.   hypothalamus
   c.   prefrontal cortex   d.   occipital cortex

5.   In a memory experiment involving recall of a series of digits, one subject reported treating the digits like phone numbers, breaking the series down into a 3-digit "area code," a 7-digit "phone number," and a 4-digit "extension." Using this procedure, the subject was able to hold 14 digits in working memory. This procedure is an example of

   a.   the method of loci   b.   semantic processing
   c.   spacing of rehearsal   d.   chunking

6.   Declarative memory can involve either _____ or _____ memory.

   a.   semantic; phonemic
   b.   semantic; structural
   c.   explicit; implicit
   d.   semantic; episodic

7.   Multiple choice tests, such as this, often involve which type of retrieval from LTM?

   a.   recognition
   b.   recall
   c.   implicit
   d.   semantic

8.   In a classical conditioning procedure in which a tone is paired with electric shock, patients with an intact hippocampus but a damaged amygdala

   a.   have no conscious idea that the tone is associated with shock, but show a conditioned fear response to it nonetheless
   b.   consciously know that the tone is associated with shock, and show a conditioned fear response to it
   c.   consciously know that the tone is associated with shock, but show no conditioned fear response to it
   d.   have no conscious idea that the tone is associated with shock, nor show a conditioned fear response to it

9.   Melanie ties a string around her finger in the morning, so she won't forget to pick up a loaf of bread on her way home from work. What aspect of memory is involved in this situation?

   a.   working memory
   b.   procedural memory
   c.   implicit memory
   d.   prospective memory

10.   Many students report that it is much easier for them to recall information when they write an in-class test in the same room as they take a the course than when they write the final examination in an examination hall or the gym. A possible reason for this difference is

   a.   interference
   b.   retrieval cues
   c.   motivated forgetting
   d.   memory decay

11.   Driving to school, Maria was mentally rehearsing for her psychology exam. To help remember the important topics for the exam, she created a ridiculous mental image of the topics being scattered around her bedroom -- on the bed, under the pillow, under the bed, on her desk, and so on. As she drove along, she suddenly realized that she had driven 3 miles without even paying attention to her driving. Yet she had not run any red lights, and she had used her clutch properly and not stalled while shifting gears. This unconscious, automatic behavior could be described as involving

    a.   declarative memory
    b.   implicit memory
    c.   episodic memory
    d.   short-term memory

12.   Maria's method of trying to remember the important topics for her exam, in the previous question, involves using

    a.   the method of loci
    b.   the SQ3R method
    c.   the deep processing method
    d.   none of the above

13.   The "spacing effect" refers to

    a.   the superiority of memory for information at both the beginning and end of a series
    b.   the superiority of memory for information rehearsed over long intervals
    c.   the superiority of memory for information broken down into chunks
    d.   the *lunch counter* model of STM – there is "limited space" at the counter

14.   Pieces of information along a network of associations are called _____.

    a.   nodes
    b.   loci
    c.   files
    d.   schemas

15.   Schemas play an important role in helping to process new information and enter it into memory. Schemas can also result in processing and retrieval errors. Which of the following errors could be attributable to schemas?

    a.   leading people to misclassify information
    b.   causing people to believe they have seen information that really was not present
    c.   causing people to fail to notice information that might be important
    d.   all of the above

16. Research on forgetting shows that

    a. forgetting follows a typical pattern with a gradual initial loss of information, with the rate of loss increasing with time
    b. the pace at which information is forgotten is quite different when the time period is hours than when the time period is years
    c. forgetting follows a typical pattern with a rapid initial loss of information, and only a gradual loss thereafter
    d. all of the above

17. Manal remembers sitting with her brother in the living room of her parents' home, wearing her pajamas, when she saw the space shuttle Columbia disaster on TV. Such vivid memories of exciting or highly consequential events are referred to as

    a. iconic memories   b. flashbulb memories
    c. retrospective memories   d. implicit memories

18. Dave's voice-mail at the office uses different number keys to play, save, or delete messages than his voice-mail at home. Dave found it very hard to use his office voice-mail. "It just doesn't make sense," he said. "I didn't have this much trouble learning my voice-mail at home. But now I can't get the numbers straight at all!" This problem where previously stored memories interfere with the retrieval of new information is called

    a. retroactive interference
    b. motivated forgetting
    c. proactive interference
    d. state-dependent learning

19. Dave finally learned the new voice-mail at the office. But now, he sometimes can't remember the numbers for his voice-mail at home. This problem, where new information interferes with retrieval of old information, is due to

    a. retroactive interference
    b. repression
    c. proactive interference
    d. state-dependent learning

20. _____ refers to the process of explicitly instructing yourself to forget ("Oops, forget that. That's the wrong address. The right address is …").

    a. proactive interference
    b. memory decay
    c. repression
    d. motivated forgetting

ANSWERS

FILL-IN EXERCISES

1. ½ , two   2. echoic 3. short-term 4. 20, 30   5. seven; five, nine   6. maintenance; elaborative
7. retrieval 8. serial position 9. nodules 10. working   11. visual; verbal; central executive
12. prefrontal cortex 13. chunking 14. declarative 15. generic 16. episodic 17. implicit   18. hippocampus
19. prospective   20. depth (or level)   21. encoding specificity   22. mnemonic; loci 23. nodes
24. hierarchically   25. schemas 26. flashbulb memories   27. decay   28. proactive

USING WHAT YOU HAVE LEARNED

This involves long-term memory. Schemas are likely responsible for the addition of the new information. Schemas tend to render the environment predictable and, without them, efficient memory would be impossible.

APPLICATION

1.   Yes. Use mnemonic devices such as *loci* method and *peg* method.

2.   Yes. Space rehearsal over a period of time.

3.   Don't just read notes over and over. Use encoding strategies. Form associative links to previously stored information. Elaborate and reflect upon the information (depth of processing). Use a variety of representational modes and mnemonic devices (especially try SQ3R method).

4.   Yes. Serial position effects

5.   Yes. The problem is retroactive interference.

SAMPLE TEST QUESTIONS

1.	c	11.	b
2.	b	12.	a
3.	a	13.	b
4.	c	14.	a
5.	d	15.	d
6.	d	16.	c
7.	a	17.	b
8.	c	18.	c
9.	d	19.	a
10.	b	20.	d

Chapter 7
Thought and Language

PART ONE: PRE-READ AND WORK
Outline and Learning Objectives

Pre-read this chapter's table of contents and end-of-chapter summary. Then, use the outline segment-by-segment to help you work through the chapter. Jot down your own questions, comments, and notes in the space provided. Make a note of difficult areas that you will need to review (include page numbers). Then, answer the questions in the learning objectives section that follows. Check off those you are confident that you can answer well. Re-read the material in the text for the questions about which you are less confident. Record the important points from your reading in the space below each question.

OUTLINE

Units of Thought

Manipulating Mental Representations

Concepts and Categories

A Global Vista: Culture and Categorization

Reasoning, Problem Solving, and Decision Making

Reasoning

Problem Solving

Decision Making

Implicit and Everyday Thinking

How Rational are We?

Implicit Cognition

Emotion, Motivation, and Decision Making

Connectionism

From Brain to Behavior: The Neuropsychology of Thinking

Language

Language and Thought

Transforming Sounds and Symbols into Meaning

The Use of Language in Everyday Life

One Step Further: Is Language Distinctly Human?

LEARNING OBJECTIVES

Upon completion of Chapter 7, you should be able to answer the following questions.

1. How does thinking employ mental images and mental models?

2. What are the differences between the defining features and prototype views of categorization?

3. How do basic, subordinate, and superordinate level categories differ?

4. Is categorization influenced by culture?

5. What are the differences between inductive reasoning and deductive reasoning?

6. How can analogical reasoning be used to help understand a novel situation?

7. What is the difference between well-defined and ill-defined problems?

8. What are the four steps involved in problem solving?

9.   Describe how algorithms and mental simulation can be used as problem-solving strategies.

10.   In what ways do functional fixedness and confirmation bias interfere with problem solving?

11.   How can the utility and probability of options be combined in the process of decision making?

12.   What are heuristics, and in what ways can they lead to irrational judgments?

13.   What is meant by the notion of bounded rationality?

14.   Explain how both learning and problem-solving can occur implicitly – that is, outside of awareness.

15.   How is prospect theory related to the way people assess risks?

16.   What is meant by the notions parallel and distributed in parallel distributed processing (PDP) models?

17.   Explain the process of parallel constraint satisfaction.

18.   Describe the consequences of damage to the dorsolateral and the ventromedial prefrontal cortex.

19.   What is the Whorfian hypothesis of linguistic relativity?

20. How do morphemes differ from phonemes?

21. How do listeners employ information about both syntax and semantics to understand the meaning of sentences?

22. How do people mentally represent discourse at multiple levels?

23 How is communication influenced both by shared rules of conversation as well as by nonverbal signals?

24. What does research with chimps reveal about the notion that language is unique to humans?

PART TWO: REVIEW AND LEARN
Key Terms, Fill-In Exercises, Application and Using What You Have Learned

Before doing the exercises below, review the information you learned in this chapter. Reread the work you did in part one of this study guide chapter, plus the interim summaries and end-of-chapter summary in your textbook. Review any problem areas. Once you feel comfortable with the material, do the following exercises without referring to your notes or textbook. If you have difficulty with a term or question, mark it and come back to it. When you have finished an exercise, go back to your notes and the textbook to find the answers to the questions that gave you difficulty. Finally, check your answers (key terms against the textbook and the rest against the answer key).

KEY TERMS

Upon completion of Chapter 7, you should be able to define the following terms.

Thinking _____

_____

Mental images _____

_____

Mental models _____

_____

Categories _____

_____

Concept _____

_____

Categorization _____

_____

Defining features _____

_____

Well-defined concepts   _____

_____

Prototype   _____

_____

Basic level   _____

_____

Subordinate level   _____

_____

Superordinate level   _____

_____

Reasoning   _____

_____

Inductive reasoning   _____

_____

Deductive reasoning   _____

_____

Syllogism   _____

_____

Analogical reasoning   _____

_____

Problem solving _____

_____

Well-defined problems   _____

_____

Ill-defined problems   _____

_____

Subgoals   _____

_____

Problem-solving strategies   _____

_____

Algorithms   _____

_____

Mental simulation   _____

_____

Functional fixedness   _____

_____

Confirmation bias   _____

_____

Decision making   _____

_____

Weighted utility value   _____

_____

Expected utility   _____

_____

Explicit cognition   _____

_____

Heuristics   _____

_____

Representativeness heuristic   _____

_____

Availability heuristic   _____

_____

Bounded rationality   _____

_____

Implicit cognition   _____

_____

Connectionism (or parallel distributed processing models) _____

_____

Constraint satisfaction   _____

_____

Dorsolateral prefrontal cortex   _____

_____

Ventromedial prefrontal cortex   _____

_____

Language   _____

_____

Whorfian hypothesis of linguistic relativity_____

_____

Phonemes   _____

_____

Morphemes   _____

_____

Phrases   _____

_____

Sentences   _____

_____

Syntax _____

_____

Grammar   _____

_____

Semantics   _____

_____

Pragmatics   _____

_____

Discourse   _____

_____

Nonverbal communication   _____

_____

FILL-IN EXERCISES

Fill in the word or words that best fit in the spaces below.

1. _____ means manipulating mental representations for a purpose.

2. _____ _____ are representations that describe, explain, or predict the way things work.

3. The process of identifying an object as an instance of a category – recognizing its similarity to some objects and dissimilarity to others – is called _____.

4. Qualities that are essential, or necessarily present, in order to classify an object as a member of a category are referred to as _____ _____.

5. A _____ is an abstraction across many instances of a category.

6. The level that people naturally tend to use in categorizing objects is known as the _____ level. The level of categorization below this is the _____ level.

7. _____ refers to the process by which people generate and evaluate arguments and beliefs.

8. Reasoning that draws a conclusion from a set of assumptions or premises is referred to as _____ reasoning.

9. A _____ consists of two premises that lead to a logical conclusion.

10. The process by which people understand a novel situation in terms of a familiar one is referred to as _____ reasoning.

11. In a well-defined problem, the _____ state, _____ state, and the _____ are easily determined.

12. _____ are systematic procedures that inevitably produce a solution to a problem.

13. Mental _____ is a problem-solving strategy that involves imagining the steps involved in solving a problem mentally before actually undertaking them.

14. _____ _____ is a common error in problem solving, in which people tend to search for confirmation of what they already believe.

15. According to information-processing models, when people make decisions, they consider the _____ as well as the _____ of the outcomes of different options.

16. In decision making, a weighted _____ _____ refers to a combined measure of the importance of an attribute and the extent to which a given option satisfies it.

17. The _____ heuristic assumes that events or occurrences that can be recalled easily must be common and are therefore likely to happen.

18. "Aha" experiences, when people set aside a seemingly insoluble problem only to find hours or days later that the answer suddenly comes to them, are examples of _____ problem solving.

19. _____ asserts that most cognitive processes occur simultaneously through the action of multiple activated networks.

20. Damage to the _____ prefrontal cortex can result in difficulty connecting feelings with thought, to make sound decisions.

21. The smallest units of sound that constitute speech are called _____, while the smallest units of meaning in a language are called _____.

22. _____ are groups of words that act as a unit and convey a meaning.

23. _____ refers to the rules that govern the placement of words and phrases in a sentence.

24. Chomsky views _____ as a system for generating acceptable language utterances and identifying those that are unacceptable.

25. Psychologists are interested in the _____ of language – that is, the way language is used and understood in everyday life.

26. People communicate through language, but they also communicate _____ through a variety of signals, including gestures, body language, touch, physical distance, facial expressions, and so on.

USING WHAT YOU HAVE LEARNED

In Chapter 7 you read about how language and thought are interconnected. In fact, some psychologists have stressed the role of self-directed communication in problem solving. Pay attention to your own problem-solving processes. Have you ever found yourself talking to yourself as you go through a problem step by step? Is it more likely to happen when you're all by yourself than with other people? Even if you don't talk out loud to yourself, do you ever talk to yourself "in your head?" Try to imagine thinking or problem solving without the use of language. What some examples of the ways in which you think without the use of language?

APPLICATION

For each of the following situations, identify the aspect of reasoning or problem solving that is illustrated.

1. Fred has taken his lucky rabbit's foot to the last three Dodgers' games, and they've won all three. He concludes that it's because of his rabbit's foot and vows to bring it to every game from now on. He remembers bringing it to the two other games he attended, and they won both times. He overlooks the fact that they've won almost every game at home this season, even though he's only been to five. What type of reasoning led Dave to his conclusion about the rabbit's foot? What type of bias is leading to Dave's erroneous conclusion?

2. When Nancy came over to Dave's for dinner, she was surprised that he was such a good cook. "Men can't cook," reasoned Nancy. "Dave is a man; therefore, Dave can't cook." What type of reasoning led Nancy to this conclusion?

3. Jane just can't forget the news report she saw on the big plane crash at the airport in her city. Ever since then, she won't fly anywhere. "Too much chance of a crash," Jane reasons. "Driving's much safer!" What led to this error in Jane's reasoning?

4. In screening new candidates for executive positions, Acme Tire company presents them with an Acme tire and asks them to come up with all possible uses for it that they can think of.

    "That's easy," says Geoff, a candidate for the position, "Put it on a car's wheels."
    The interviewer replies, "And what else could you use it for?"
    "On a truck's wheels," says Geoff, hesitatingly.
    "Anything else?" questions the interviewer.
    "I know!" says Geoff, proud of his ingenuity, "A trailer's wheels!"

    What limitation underlies Geoff's difficulty with the question?

PART THREE: TEST AND KNOW
SAMPLE TEST QUESTIONS

Test how well you have learned this chapter's material by answering the sample test questions. You may wish to mark your answers on a separate sheet of paper so you can reuse this test for exam review. Once you have completed the exam, check your answers and then go back to your notes and the textbook to review questions you found difficult.

1.   A mental representation of a category (i.e., an internal portrait of a class of objects, ideas, or events that share common properties) is referred to as a

    a.   concept   b.   mental image
    c.   mental model   d.   prototype

2.   The concept "adult" is a good example of a(n)

    a.   well-defined concept
    b.   inductive category
    c.   basic level category
    d.   none of the above

3.   A prototype is

    a.   a visual representation, such as an image or a geometric form
    b.   a representation of a system that enables people to describe, explain, and predict how things work
    c.   a mental representation of a class of objects, ideas, or events that share common properties
    d.   an abstraction across many instances of a category

4.   Referring to robins, blue jays, and penguins as "animals" is an example of

    a.   the basic level of categorization
    b.   the superordinate level of categorization
    c.   the defining features method of categorization
    d.   the prototype-matching method of categorization

5.   "It snows in winter. Since there is snow on the ground, then it must be winter."
    This type of reasoning is called

    a.   inductive reasoning
    b.   deductive reasoning
    c.   implicit problem solving
    d.   decision making

6.   Bill has noticed that almost every time he shakes hands with someone who has a cold, he comes down with a cold, too. He concludes that the cold virus can be transmitted via hand-to-hand contact. This reasoning is an example of

a.	problem solving	b.	hypothesis testing
c.	inductive reasoning	d.	deductive reasoning

7.   Your friend's mother claims that she was unable to program the VCR to record a favorite TV program until it was explained to her in terms of how she usually programs the timer on the oven to cook a chicken while she is at work. This is an example of

a.   deductive reasoning
b.   analogical reasoning
c.   syllogistic reasoning
d.   inductive reasoning

8.   Which of the following is not a feature of the problem-solving process?

a.   identify the initial state
b.   select an operator
c.   establish superordinate goals
d.   identify the goal state

9.   Dave and Nancy sent out 100 invitations to their wedding. They then took the number of replies they received and multiplied them by the price per plate that the caterer had given, to arrive at the cost of the wedding reception dinner. This problem-solving strategy is an example of a(n)

a.	algorithm	b.	syllogism
c.	heuristic	d.	prototype

10.   The process of weighing the pros and cons of different alternatives before making a choice is called

a.	critical thinking	b.	decision making
c.	inductive reasoning	d.	deductive reasoning

11.   According to one information-processing model, when people make decisions, they consider two things:

a.   the representativeness of a particular outcome and the frequency with which it has occurred in the past
b.   the pragmatic value of the decision and the difficulty involved in solving the problem
c.   the inclusiveness and the size of the category
d.   the utility of the outcomes of different outcomes and the probability of each outcome

12.   Prospect theory is a theory of decision making that

   a.   suggests that the value of future losses is more important to people than that of future gains
   b.   describes the tendency to settle on a cognitive solution that has the prospect of satisfying as many constraints as possible
   c.   suggests that the prospect of gain is more important in people's choices than the potential for loss
   d.   the prospect of making an irrational choice tends to greatly impede people's ability to make good choices

13.   When the fan belt broke on her car, Melanie pulled out a pair of nylons from her shopping bag and told Gord: "This will fix it!" Gord just couldn't see how you could use nylons for anything other than wearing. Gord's problem is known as

   a.   the representativeness heuristic
   b.   the availability heuristic
   c.   the confirmation bias
   d.   functional fixedness

14.   After his boss won the $10 million jackpot in the national lottery, Malcolm bought 10 tickets for the next draw, thinking his chances must be pretty good of winning. This reasoning is an example of

   a.   the representativeness heuristic
   b.   the availability heuristic
   c.   the confirmation bias
   d.   functional fixedness

15.   After spending the morning trying to solve a problem, Mazen decided to forget it. That night, while lying in bed, the answer suddenly came to him. This is an example of

   a.   reasoning by analogy
   b.   deductive reasoning
   c.   decision making
   d.   implicit problem solving

16.   Connectionist models differ from traditional information-processing models in that the underlying metaphor is no longer really "mind as computer." Rather it is mind as

   a.   a set of algorithms functioning in series
   b.   a set of heuristics involved in problem solving
   c.   a set of neurons that activate and inhibit one another
   d.   the programmer of the computer

17. Damage to the _____ is associated with impaired planning, distractibility, and deficits in working memory.

    a. dorsolateral prefrontal cortex
    b. ventrolateral prefrontal cortex
    c. ventromedial prefrontal cortex
    d. dorsomedial prefrontal cortex

18. According to the Whorfian hypothesis of linguistic relativity

    a. languages all have the same relative function from one culture to another
    b. the frequency of word use is relative within a given language
    c. language shapes thought
    d. thought shapes language

19. The suffix "ed," added to a verb to make the past tense, is an example of

    a. syntax
    b. pragmatics
    c. a morpheme
    d. decision making

20. The pragmatics of language is concerned with

    a. the way people ordinarily speak, hear, read, and write in interconnected sentences
    b. the way language is used and understood in everyday life
    c. the rules that govern the placement of words and phrases in a sentence
    d. the rules that govern the meanings of morphemes, words, phrases, and sentences

ANSWERS

FILL-IN EXERCISES

1. thinking   2. mental models   3. categorization   4. defining features   5. prototype   6. basic; subordinate
7. reasoning   8. deductive   9. syllogism   10. analogical   11. initial; goal; operators   12. algorithms
13. simulation   14. confirmation bias   15. utility; probability   16. utility value   17. availability   18. implicit
19. connectionism (or parallel distributed processing)   20. ventromedial   21. phonemes; morphemes
22. phrases   23. syntax   24. grammar   25. pragmatics   26. nonverbally

APPLICATION

1. inductive reasoning; confirmation bias
2. deductive reasoning (a syllogism)
3. availability heuristic
4. functional fixedness

SAMPLE TEST QUESTIONS

1.	a	11.	d
2.	d	12.	a
3.	d	13.	d
4.	b	14.	a
5.	b	15.	d
6.	c	16.	c
7.	b	17.	a
8.	c	18.	c
9.	a	19.	c
10.	b	20.	b

Chapter 8
Intelligence

PART ONE: PRE-READ AND WORK
Outline and Learning Objectives

Pre-read this chapter's table of contents and end-of-chapter summary. Then, use the outline segment-by-segment to help you work through the chapter. Jot down your own questions, comments, and notes in the space provided. Make a note of difficult areas that you will need to review (include page numbers). Then, answer the questions in the learning objectives section that follows. Check off those you are confident that you can answer well. Re-read the material in the text for the questions about which you are less confident. Record the important points from your reading in the space below each question.

OUTLINE

The Nature of Intelligence

Intelligence is Multifaceted and Functional

A Global Vista: The Cultural Context of Intelligence

Intelligence Testing

Binet's Scale

Intelligence Testing Crosses the Atlantic

One Step Further: The extremes of Intelligence

From Brain to Behavior: Is Bigger Better?

Validity and Limitations of IQ tests

Approaches to Intelligence

The Psychometric Approach

The Information-Processing Approach

A Theory of Multiple Intelligences

Heredity and Intelligence

From Brain to Behavior: Individual Differences in IQ

Group Differences: Race and Intelligence

Commentary: The Science and Politics of Intelligence

LEARNING OBJECTIVES

Upon completion of Chapter 8, you should be able to answer the following questions.

1.   What three questions are central to understanding intelligence?

2.   Explain how intelligence can be viewed as culturally defined.

3.   How did the efforts of Alfred Binet and those of Sir Francis Galton differ?

4.   What is meant by the concept of mental age, introduced by Binet and Simon in 1908?

5.   On the Stanford-Binet Scale (1916), how was an intelligence quotient or IQ score calculated?

6.   What were David Wechsler's contributions to modern-day intelligence testing procedures?

7.   How is mental retardation defined, and what are some of its possible causes?

8.   What is "giftedness?"

9.   How can creativity be measured, and how is this attribute related to intelligence?

10.   Is brain size related to intelligence?

11.   Discuss the following criticisms and controversies that surround IQ testing:

Lack of a theoretical basis

Possible cultural bias

Questions of validity

12.   What are Spearman's two factors, and how are they related to one another?

13.   In what ways do fluid intelligence and crystallized intelligence differ?

14.   How would a cognitive psychologist, from the information-processing approach, define intelligence?

15.   How do the following three processes underlie performance on intelligence tests, from an information-processing point of view?

Speed of processing

Knowledge base

Ability to acquire and apply cognitive strategies

16.   What are the seven intelligences identified by Howard Gardner? What criteria did he employ in choosing them?

17.   What do findings from twin, family, and adoption studies show about the influence of nature and nurture on intelligence?

18.   What has research shown concerning the issue of race and intelligence?

19.   Outline the three major conclusions of the American Psychological Association task force on intelligence and intelligence testing.

PART TWO: REVIEW AND LEARN
Key Terms, Fill-In Exercises, Application and Using What You Have Learned

Before doing the exercises below, review the information you learned in this chapter. Reread the work you did in part one of this study guide chapter, plus the interim summaries and end-of-chapter summary in your textbook. Review any problem areas. Once you feel comfortable with the material, do the following exercises without referring to your notes or textbook. If you have difficulty with a term or question, mark it and come back to it. When you have finished an exercise, go back to your notes and the textbook to find the answers to the questions that gave you difficulty. Finally, check your answers (key terms against the textbook and the rest against the answer key).

KEY TERMS

Upon completion of Chapter 8, you should be able to define the following terms.

Intelligence   _____

_____

Psychometric instruments   _____

_____

Intelligence tests   _____

_____

Mental age (MA)   _____

_____

Intelligence quotient (IQ)_____

_____

Wechsler Adult Intelligence Scale, Third Edition (WAIS-III) _____

_____

Wechsler Intelligence Scale for Children (WISC-III) _____

_____

Mental retardation _____

_____

Giftedness _____

_____

Creativity _____

_____

Divergent thinking _____

_____

Psychometric approach _____

_____

Factor analysis _____

_____

Two-factor theory of intelligence _____

_____

g-factor _____

_____

s-factors _____

_____

Gf-Gc theory _____

_____

Fluid intelligence _____

_____

Crystallized intelligence _____

_____

Knowledge base _____

_____

Theory of multiple intelligences _____

_____

FILL-IN EXERCISES

Fill in the word or words that best fit in the spaces below.

1.   In recent years, psychologists have come to recognize that intelligence is multi-_____ and
      _____.

2.   For the purpose of intelligence testing, psychologists use _____ instruments – tests that quantify
      psychological abilities such as intellectual ability – to see how people differ from and compare to
      each other on psychological "scales."

3.   Historians credit _____ of England with the first systematic effort to measure intelligence.

4.   The most direct ancestor of today's intelligence tests was developed in France, in the year 1905,
      by _____.

5.   The notion of _____ _____ refers to the average age at which children achieve a particular
      score.

6.   Lewis Terman translated into English and revised the intelligence test produced in France to
      produce the _____-_____ scale.

7.   In addition to a single, overall IQ score, the WAIS-III yields separate scores for each of the 14 subtests and overall scores for _____ and _____ IQ.

8.   David Wechsler is credited with remedying the problems associated with the concept of *mental age* by abandoning the concept, and, instead, calculating IQ as an individual's position relative to peers of the same age on a _____ distribution.

9.   Most people's scores fall within the average range, between about _____ and _____, on the IQ distribution.

10.   Roughly 2% of the American population is _____ _____, that is, significantly below average in general intellectual functioning (IQ less than _____), with deficits in adaptive behavior evident during childhood, and appear in more than one realm.

11.   _____ is a quality that is related to both intelligence and giftedness; this quality can be defined as "the ability to produce valued outcomes in a novel way."

12.   _____ thinking refers to the ability to generate multiple possibilities in a given situation.

13.   The _____ of a psychological test refers to its ability to assess the construct it was designed to measure.

14.   The primary tool of the psychometric approach to intelligence is _____ _____, a statistical procedure for identifying common elements that underlie performance across a set of tasks.

15.   Spearman proposed a two-factor theory of intelligence which distinguished two types of factors -- _____ and _____.

16.   Whereas _____ intelligence refers to people's store of knowledge, _____ intelligence refers to intellectual capacities that have no specific content but are used in processing information and approaching novel problems.

17.   According to the information-processing approach, intelligence is best defined as a _____ rather than as a measurable quantity; individual differences in intelligence are assumed to reflect differences in the _____ operations people use in thinking.

18.   According to the information-processing approach, individual differences in intellectual functioning may reflect differences in processing _____, in knowledge _____, and in ability to acquire and apply cognitive _____.

19.   Howard Gardner's theory of _____ intelligences grounds intelligence in both its _____ and cultural context.

20.   Gardner's theory identifies seven intelligences: _____, _____, _____, _____, _____, _____, and _____.

21. The logic of _____, _____, and _____ studies, in distinguishing some of the influences of nature and nurture on intelligence, is to examine subjects whose genetic relatedness is known and to see whether or not degree of genetic relatedness predicts the size of the correlation between their IQs.

22. The results of the Texas Adoption Project, like the findings of several other studies, suggest that although genes and environment both influence IQ in childhood, the impact of the family environment _____ (*increases/decreases*) with age, as the impact of genetics _____ (*increases/decreases*).

APPLICATION

1. A friend of yours has just watched a television talk show that focused on the IQ and race controversy. This is the first time your friend has ever heard about IQ differences between racial groups, and the whole issue has left her rather confused. Knowing that you're studying the topic of intelligence in your psychology course, she turns to you to provide answers to some of her questions. Her major question is whether intelligence is inherited or is the consequence of the environment in which a person grows up. Drawing on findings from twin, family, and adoption studies that you've read about in Chapter 8, what would you tell her concerning the relative roles of heredity and environment in both individual and group differences in IQ?

2. A friend who is a parent has just been told that her child has been identified as "*gifted*." She has lots of questions about what giftedness means. Because she knows that you've been studying the topic of intelligence, your friend asks what you can tell her about giftedness. She wonders whether giftedness is related to IQ. She's also heard, however, that giftedness has something to do with creativity and wonders how IQ and creativity may be related. Finally, she's heard stories that gifted children may grow up unhappy and socially maladjusted. From what you've read in Chapter 8, how would you answer her questions and concerns?

3. Two psychology students are discussing the criticism that IQ tests may be culturally biased. After examining sample questions from several popular IQ tests, they conclude that the biggest problem is questions that are heavily language-based and assess general knowledge. They propose developing a "*culture-free*" test that does not require language and does not assess general knowledge. Instead, their test would measure intelligence in terms of how quickly people can sort abstract geometrical shapes. They're convinced that their test couldn't possible be culturally biased. Based on what you've read in Chapter 8, do you agree? Why or why not?

USING WHAT YOU HAVE LEARNED

A senior in high school, Jeffrey almost didn't come to school today, at all. This morning his parents dropped a bombshell: They're getting a divorce! Coming as a complete shock, this news had a profound effect on Jeffrey, making him upset, confused, and sad. It's as if all of a sudden his whole world has been turned upside down. To make matters worse, today is the day that the Scholastic Aptitude Test (SAT) is being administered at Jeffrey's school. Being a straight A student, Jeffrey plans to attend college in the fall. His marks on the SAT will, to a large extent, influence whether or not he will be accepted into the college of his choice.

If you were a close friend of Jeffrey would you recommend that he write the SAT today? Why or why not? If Jeffrey decides to write the SAT, what effect might his present emotional state have on his test scores? If, during the test, Jeffrey is especially anxious to get home and talk things over with his parents, is this likely to make matters worse? Why or why not?

PART THREE: TEST AND KNOW
SAMPLE TEST QUESTIONS

Test how well you have learned this chapter's material by answering the sample test questions. You may wish to mark your answers on a separate sheet of paper so you can reuse this test for exam review. Once you have completed the exam, check your answers and then go back to your notes and the textbook to review questions you found difficult.

1.   Intelligence is functional. From an evolutionary perspective,

   a.   people use their intelligence to satisfy wishes and avoid things they fear.
   b.   intelligent behavior solves problems of adaptation and hence facilitates survival and reproduction.
   c.   intelligence is applied cognition, using cognitive skills to solve problems or obtain desired ends.
   d.   all of the above.

2.   Western views of intelligence typically emphasize:

   a.   verbal ability, and mathematical and spatial abilities
   b.   verbal ability, practical abilities, and competencies
   c.   personal qualities, skills, and cognitive style
   d   independence, alertness, and verbal skills

3. History will remember _____, not only as the first to attempt to test mental abilities, but also as a pioneering statistician who discovered how to express the relationship between two variables (such as the intelligence of one member of a twin pair with that of the other) using _____ _____.

    a. Galton; the correlation coefficient
    b. Binet; the correlation coefficient
    c. Binet; factor analysis
    d. Spearman; factor analysis

4. As proposed by Lewis Terman, which of the following formulas *correctly* expresses the intelligence quotient (IQ) as the relation between an individual's mental age (MA) and chronological age (CA) ?

    a. IQ = (MA/CA) ÷ 100
    b. IQ = (CA/MA) ÷100
    c. IQ = (MA/CA) X100
    d. IQ = (CA/MA) X100

5. If the question *"How are a nickel and a quarter alike?"* were asked as part of the WAIS-III, it would most likely be included as an item in the _____ subtest.

    a. Comprehension
    b. Performance
    c. Arithmetic
    d. Similarities

6. In the United States, approximately what percentage of individuals who are mentally handicapped are classified as severely to profoundly retarded?

    a. 2 %   b. 75 to 90%
    c. 1% or less   d. 10%

7. PKU

    a. is a highly heritable condition that can, however, be treated by dietary restrictions
    b. is a disorder most frequently caused by an extra chromosome
    c. frequently results from exposure of the fetus to alcohol early in pregnancy
    d. is often associated with poverty and other similar psychosocial causes

8. In Western society, with its emphasis on academic aptitude as measured by psychometric tests, giftedness is most often equated with

    a. an IQ that is above average   b. an IQ exceeding 130
    c. an IQ exceeding 200   d. creativity

9.   One strategy for assessing creativity is to measure _____ thinking. This type of thinking involves generating multiple possibilities from a given situation, such as describing all the possible uses of a paper clip.

a.   fluid   b.   functional
c.   divergent   d.   savant

10.   As determined by intelligence tests, IQ is _____ related to school grades, showing a correlation coefficient of between _____ and _____.

a.   mildly; .60, .70   b.   strongly; .90, 1.0
c.   strongly; .60, .70   d.   mildly; .12, .20

11.   For many years, critics have argued that intelligence tests

a.   lack a theoretical basis
b.   fail to capture the type of practical intelligence involved in achieving goals in every day life
c.   are culturally biased
d.   all of the above

12.   IQ tests place individuals on a continuum of intelligence, but, in general, they do *not*

a.   provide an overall IQ score
b.   explain what intelligence is
c.   quantify intellectual functioning in a way that allows comparison among individuals
d.   predict school success

13.   Spearman's theory of intelligence

a.   attempts to explain the specific cognitive processes that underlie intelligent behavior
b.   dates back to 1857
c.   distinguishes the g-factor, or general intelligence, from s-factors, or specific abilities
d.   contends that highly intelligent people do not tend to be maladjusted

14.   The Gf-Gc theory distinguishes two general factors of _____ and _____ intelligence.

a.   verbal; performance
b.   fluid, crystallized
c.   general; specific
d.   all of the above

15.   In contrast to the psychometric approach, which tries to _____ basic abilities, the information-processing approach tries to understand the specific _____ that underlie intelligent behavior.

a.   complicate; attitudes   b.   adapt; structure
c.   quantify; processes   d.   none of the above

16.   Which of the following three variables have been identified by information-processing theorists as being particularly important in explaining individual differences in intelligence?

    a.   speed of processing; memory strategies; fluid abilities
    b.   knowledge base; divergent thinking patterns; ability to acquire and apply mental strategies
    c.   memory strategies; fluid abilities; divergent thinking patterns
    d.   speed of processing; knowledge base; ability to acquire and apply mental strategies

17.   Which of the following was *not* identified as a type of intelligence by Howard Gardner in his theory of multiple intelligences?

    a.   reasoning   b.   logical/mathematical
    c.   musical   d.   bodily/kinesthetic

18.   Gardner argues that intelligences can be isolated based on a number of criteria, including

    a.   their neurological similarity, the presence of savants, and their similar courses of development
    b.   their neurological independence, the presence of savants, and their different courses of development
    c.   their neurological independence, the presence of savants, and their similar courses of development
    d.   their neurological similarity, the presence of savants, and their different courses of development

19.   A longitudinal study examining the relation between a child's IQ at age 4 and 13 and the number of risk factors to which the child was exposed showed that:

    a.   the child's IQ varied directly with the number of risk factors: the more risk factors, the higher the child's IQ
    b.   the number of risk factors to which the child was exposed was unrelated to the child's IQ
    c   environmental variables have little or no effect on individual differences in intelligence
    d   the child's IQ varied inversely with the number of risk factors: the more risk factors, the lower the child's IQ

20.   Which of the following is consistent with the conclusions of the American Psychological Association task force on intelligence and intelligence testing?

    a.   IQ tests are highly predictive of school success
    b.   The heritability of IQ is highest in children, but declines as people approach adulthood.
    c.   IQ tests are biased against particular groups: they predict outcomes such as school performance between groups, but not within groups.
    d.   all of the above

ANSWERS

FILL-IN EXERCISES

1. faceted; functional   2. psychometric   3. Sir Francis Galton   4. Alfred Binet   5. mental age
6. Stanford-Binet   7. verbal; performance   8. frequency   9. 85; 115   10. mentally retarded; 70
11. creativity   12. divergent   13. validity   14. factor analysis   15. general (or g-factor); specific (or s-factors)
16. crystallized; fluid   17. process; cognitive   18. speed; base; strategies   19. multiple; neurological
20. musical; bodily/kinesthetic; spatial; linguistic or verbal; logical/mathematical; intrapersonal;
interpersonal   21. twin, family, adoption   22. decreases; increases

APPLICATION

1.   Twin, family, and adoption studies show that *both* heredity and environment play important roles in influencing intelligence. While genetic factors may account for many of the observed individual differences in IQ, environmental factors likely account for differences between groups. The analogy of differences in the size of military uniforms from different eras helps explain these differences.

2.   Giftedness is frequently defined as IQ exceeding 130, although common definitions extend to other forms of talent such as social, musical, or athletic ability. Creativity, a quality related to giftedness, is only moderately correlated with intelligence. Terman's research suggests that gifted individuals tend to have average or above-average adjustment, slightly better chances of marital success, and far greater likelihood of achieving vocational success than the general population.

3.   The students are incorrect. Both sorting abstract geometric shapes and the emphasis on speed in their test can be culturally biased.

SAMPLE TEST QUESTIONS

1.	b	11.	d
2.	a	12.	b
3.	a	13.	c
4.	c	14.	b
5.	d	15.	c
6.	d	16.	d
7.	a	17.	a
8.	b	18.	b
9.	c	19.	d
10.	c	20.	a

Chapter 9
Consciousness

PART ONE: PRE-READ AND WORK
Outline and Learning Objectives

Pre-read this chapter's table of contents and end-of-chapter summary. Then, use the outline segment-by-segment to help you work through the chapter. Jot down your own questions, comments, and notes in the space provided. Make a note of difficult areas that you will need to review (include page numbers). Then, answer the questions in the learning objectives section that follows. Check off those you are confident that you can answer well. Re-read the material in the text for the questions about which you are less confident. Record the important points from your reading in the space below each question.

OUTLINE

The Nature of Consciousness

Functions of Consciousness

Consciousness and Attention

Perspectives on Consciousness

The Psychodynamic Unconscious

The Cognitive Unconscious

Commentary: An Integrated View of Consciousness

From Brain to Behavior: The Neuropsychology of Consciousness

Sleep and Dreaming

The Nature and Evolution of Sleep

Stages of Sleep

Three Views of Dreaming

Altered States of Consciousness

Meditation

Hypnosis

One Step Further: Is Hypnosis Real?

Drug-Induced States of Consciousness

A Global Vista: Religious Experiences in Cross-Cultural Perspective

LEARNING OBJECTIVES

Upon completion of Chapter 9, you should be able to answer the following questions.

1.   Discuss the two primary functions of consciousness -- monitor and control.

2.   Identify and discuss the three functions of attention.

3.   How have researchers examined the phenomenon of divided attention?

4.   According to Freud, what three mental systems comprise consciousness?

5.   Can unconscious motivation influence behavior?

6.   How do cognitive psychologists view conscious and unconscious processes?

7.   What insights do the disorders of split brains and amnesia reveal concerning the neuropsychology of consciousness?

8.   What neural structures are involved in the experience of consciousness?

9.   What are circadian rhythms and how are they controlled? What are the consequences of disrupting an individual's circadian rhythms?

10.   What are the effects of extreme sleep deprivation?

11.   How can individuals avoid or reduce insomnia?

12.   Describe each of the four stages of sleep.

13.   How do REM and NREM sleep differ?

14.   What are the similarities and differences in the psychodynamic, cognitive, and biological views of the nature and significance of dreaming?

15.   What is meant by the term "altered states of consciousness"?

16.   What are the characteristics of meditation?

17.   What are the characteristics of hypnosis?

18.   Discuss the controversy over the use of hypnosis to retrieve forgotten memories.

19.   Is hypnosis real? Consider this question from two different perspectives: (a) that of a skeptic, and (b) that of an advocate of hypnosis.

20.   What are the effects of alcohol and other depressants?

21.   How are the effects of alcohol influenced by expectations?

22.   What are the consequences of alcohol use and abuse?

23.   Identify four stimulant drugs and describe their effects.

24.   What are the effects, both immediate and chronic, of hallucinogenic drug use?

25.   What are the effects of marijuana use?

26.   In what ways might religious experiences be considered altered states of consciousness?

PART TWO: REVIEW AND LEARN
Key Terms, Fill-In Exercises, Application and Using What You Have Learned

Before doing the exercises below, review the information you learned in this chapter. Reread the work you did in part one of this study guide chapter, plus the interim summaries and end-of-chapter summary in your textbook. Review any problem areas. Once you feel comfortable with the material, do the following exercises without referring to your notes or textbook. If you have difficulty with a term or question, mark it and come back to it. When you have finished an exercise, go back to your notes and the textbook to find the answers to the questions that gave you difficulty. Finally, check your answers (key terms against the textbook and the rest against the answer key).

KEY TERMS

Upon completion of Chapter 9, you should be able to define the following terms.

States of consciousness _____

_____

Consciousness _____

_____

Attention   _____

_____

Selective inattention _____

_____

Divided attention   _____

_____

Dichotic listening   _____

_____

Conscious mental processes _____

_____

Preconscious mental processes _____

_____

Unconscious mental processes _____

_____

Cognitive unconscious _____

_____

Circadian rhythm _____

_____

Insomnia _____

_____

Rapid eye movement (REM) sleep _____

_____

Non-REM (NREM) sleep _____

_____

Manifest content _____

_____

Latent content _____

_____

Altered states of consciousness _____

_____

Meditation   _____

_____

Hypnosis   _____

_____

Hypnotic susceptibility   _____

_____

Psychoactive substances   _____

_____

Depressants   _____

_____

Stimulants   _____

_____

Hallucinations   _____

_____

Hallucinogens   _____

_____

Religious experiences   _____

_____

FILL-IN EXERCISES

Fill in the word or words that best fit in the spaces below.

1. Two functions of consciousness are readily apparent: Consciousness _____ the self and the environment, and it _____ thought and behavior.

2. _____ refers to the process of focusing conscious awareness, providing heightened sensitivity to a limited range of experience requiring more extensive information processing.

3. Diverting attention from information that may be relevant but emotionally upsetting, a process called _____ _____, can be highly adaptive, such as ignoring anxiety while writing an exam, but can also be maladaptive, such as ignoring a darkening birthmark that could be cancerous.

4. One way researchers study divided attention is through _____ _____ tasks, in which subjects are fitted with earphones, and different information is simultaneously presented to the left and right ears.

5. According to Freud, _____ mental processes involve subjective awareness of stimuli, feelings, or ideas.

6. According to Freud unconscious processes are inaccessible to consciousness because they would be too anxiety provoking to acknowledge and thus have been _____.

7. The _____ _____ of cognitive research refers to information-processing mechanisms that operate outside awareness.

8. Information-processing models often use the terms consciousness and _____ memory interchangeably.

9. According to the cognitive perspective, _____ (*unconscious/preconscious*) cognitive processes refer to associations and schemas (declarative knowledge) activated below the threshold of consciousness that influence conscious thought and behavior.

10. People with _____ brains, whose two hemispheres function independently following severing of the corpus callosum, provide one window into the neuropsychology of consciousness.

11. Although people differ widely in the amount of sleep they need and the amount they actually get, most report sleeping _____ to _____ hours per night.

12. A _____ rhythm is a cyclical, sleep-wake biological process.

13. Researchers have recently discovered that the concentration of a modulatory neurotransmitter, called _____, increases with each additional hour and animal is awake and tends to foster sleep when an animal has been awake to long.

14.   Stage _____ sleep is marked by large, slow, rhythmic *delta* waves (less than 1 cycle per second). When delta waves comprise more than 50% of recorded brain activity, the person has entered Stage _____ sleep.

15.   Rapid eye movement (REM) sleep is called _____ because the EEG resembles the awake state.

16.   Freud distinguished between the _____ content, or story line of a dream and the _____ content, or the dream's underlying meaning.

17.   Many religions, such as Buddhism, believe that _____ leads to a deepened understanding of reality.

18.   The limits of hypnosis are _____ *(significant/insignificant)* enough that many states in the United States now _____ *(outlaw/allow)* the use of hypnotically induced memories in court testimony.

19.   _____ _____ are drugs that operate on the nervous system to alter mental activity.

20.   Psychoactive substances alter consciousness not only _____, by facilitating or inhibiting neural transmission at the synapse, but also psychologically, through _____ beliefs and expectations.

21.   Contrary to what many people who rely on alcohol to elevate their mood believe, alcohol is actually a _____.

22.   Used since about 500 AD, _____ is one of the most *potent* pleasure-inducing substances, as well as one of the most addictive, ever discovered.

23.   Hallucinogenic drug use in Europe and North America dramatically increased in the 1960s with the discovery of the synthetic hallucinogen, _____.

USING WHAT YOU HAVE LEARNED

On the bus ride home from the state fair, you overhear a young couple in the seat in front of you talking about the "Amazing Alphonso," a hypnotist all of you have just watched perform. The woman is convinced that Alphonso and his show were a hoax; she's sure that most of his "volunteers" were really actors, planted in the audience. The rest, she contends, were just "going along," performing whatever bizarre behaviors Alphonso asked them to -- from barking like a dog to kissing all of the bald men in the audience on the head. As for herself, she's convinced she could *never* be hypnotized!

Having just read about altered states of consciousness, what information might you offer to this woman about the validity of hypnosis? How would you explain the concepts of hypnotic susceptibility and posthypnotic suggestion to her?

Hearing the discussion about the Amazing Alphonso, another passenger on the bus joins in the conversation. Right away, he's recognized as one of the volunteers from the audience who participated in the show! For the last hour, you've watched this man on stage, convinced he was a 6-year-old boy playing at the beach, as he painstakingly built a huge sand castle. When Alphonso walked up and kicked the sand castle over, the man actually cried! Although he is anxious to defend his experience as legitimate, the sand castle builder can remember very little about what went on. He says he was very relaxed, but that he wasn't really conscious of what he was doing. He even acts surprised when he is told about his own behavior and that of his fellow volunteers.

Does the sand castle builder's memory of having been hypnotized seem reasonable? Why or why not? What information might you offer to him about hypnosis? How would you explain the concepts of age regression and the hidden observer?

Now that you've established yourself as the "expert" on hypnosis (on this bus, at least), your fellow passengers want to hear more about what you know. What would you tell them about the use of hypnosis in retrieving forgotten memories? What about its use by police detectives to help solve cases? Finally, how would you summarize the controversy that has surrounded hypnosis?

APPLICATION

Situation

Over the last few weeks, a friend of yours has been having a terrible time getting a good night's sleep. She lies there for hours, unable to fall asleep, just watching the night pass by on the clock beside her bed. This situation has been going on for some time, and she's really starting to worry about it. Lately, she's been so worried about not getting a good night's sleep that she can hardly sleep at all.

Questions to Answer

1. Based on what you've read about sleep, do you think your friend might be suffering from insomnia? What advice would you give her to cope with this condition?

2. Determined to "sleep-in" on a rainy Saturday morning, your friend makes the decision that – regardless when she wakes up -- she will stay in bed, *no matter what*. Is this strategy likely to help her with her problem? Why or why not?

3. In an effort to *exhaust* herself to sleep, your friend decides that she will attend a late-night high-impact aerobics class, then rush home and go to bed. Is this strategy likely to help her with her problem? Why or why not?

4. When all else fails, your friend decides that she has no other alternative but to take some of her father's sleeping pills, in order to "put an end to this vicious cycle of sleeplessness, once and for all." What advice would you give her about this decision?

PART THREE: TEST AND KNOW
SAMPLE TEST QUESTIONS

Test how well you have learned this chapter's material by answering the sample test questions. You may wish to mark your answers on a separate sheet of paper so you can reuse this test for exam review. Once you have completed the exam, check your answers and then go back to your notes and the textbook to review questions you found difficult.

1.   At any given time, people are dimly aware of

    a.   much more than what is conscious
    b.   only what is conscious
    c.   having certain painful memories repressed
    d.   preconscious and unconscious processes

2.   The *cocktail party phenomenon* suggests that

   a.   the effects of alcohol are influenced by expectations
   b.   the drugs that some young people take when "clubbing" may be dangerous because of a lack of quality control
   c.   we implicitly process much more information than reaches consciousness
   d.   alcohol can be useful in diverting attention from information that may be relevant but emotionally upsetting

3.   Splitting attention between two complex tasks is known as

   a.   split-brain attention   b.   dichotic attention
   c.   selective attention   d.   divided attention

4.   Although consciousness occupied a central role in the first textbook on psychology, when _____ came into ascendance, the study of consciousness was relegated to the periphery of psychological awareness and remained that way until the 1980s

   a.   psychoanalysis
   b.   information-processing models
   c.   behaviorism
   d.   the evolutionary perspective

5.   As defined by Freud, _____ mental processes are not presently conscious, but could be readily brought to consciousness if the need arose.

   a.   subliminal   b.   preconscious
   c.   repressed   d.   unconscious

6.   John Kihlstrom describes _____ cognitive processes as "skills or procedures that operate without awareness and are not accessible to consciousness under any circumstance."

   a.   unconscious
   b.   preconscious
   c.   independent
   d.   repressed

7.   Studies with amnesiacs have shown that people can remember things _____, even while lacking _____ memory.

   a.   over the long term; short-term
   b.   subliminally; long-term
   c.   under hypnosis; conscious
   d.   implicitly; explicit

8.   Which of the following *best* describes the relation between the number of hours that people sleep and mortality rates?

   a.   People who report sleeping for unusually short durations are prone to die earlier than are people who report sleeping eight to nine hours per night.
   b.   People who report sleeping for unusually long durations are less likely to die early than those whose sleep is closer to average, because of the restorative function of sleep.
   c.   People who report sleeping for unusually long *or* unusually short durations are prone to die earlier than those whose reported sleep is closer to average.
   d.   There is no relation between amount of sleep and mortality rates.

9.   During periods of darkness, the pineal gland produces a hormone called:

   a.   adenosine
   b.   melatonin
   c.   adrenaline
   d.   dopamine

10.   Sleep apnea refers to

   a.   a cyclical biological process that evolved around the daily cycles of light and dark
   b.   a cessation of breathing during sleep that can result in repeated wakening during the night
   c.   a possible effect of chronic use of sleeping medication
   d.   one of the consequences of prolonged use of stimulants

11.   When delta waves comprise more than 50 percent of recorded brain activity, a person has entered Stage _____ sleep.

   a.   1   b.   2
   c.   3   d.   4

12.   During a typical night's sleep, a complete cycle of REM and NREM sleep occurs about every

   _____.

   a.   90 minutes   b.   4 hours
   c.   30 minutes   d.   hour

13.   Freud proposed using free association to parts of a dream while an analyst traces the networks of association as a means to uncover:

   a.   the latent content of a dream
   b.   the manifest content of a dream
   c.   the emotional content of a dream
   d.   the dynamic content of a dream

14. As proposed by _____, dreams express current concerns of one sort or another, in a language with its own peculiar grammar. For example, the thought, " I am worried about my upcoming exam," might be translated into a dream about falling off a cliff.

    a. Freud
    b. Korsakoff
    c. Foulkes
    d. Kihlstrom

15. People who are _____ tend to be able to form vivid visual images and to become readily absorbed in fantasy, daydreams, movies, and the like.

    a. highly susceptible to REM sleep
    b. high in hypnotic susceptibility
    c. quite able to develop a deep state of tranquility by altering their normal flow of conscious thoughts
    d. highly susceptible to the effects of psychoactive substances

16. Cross-culturally, the most widely used psychoactive substance is

    a. LSD
    b. cocaine
    c. marijuana
    d. alcohol

17. In the United States, approximately one in _____ people abuse alcohol, and another one in _____ misuse other psychoactive substances.

    a. five; seven
    b. seven; twenty
    c. twenty; fifty
    d. ten; twenty

18. Which of the following is *not* an example of a stimulant?

    a. cocaine
    b. nicotine
    c. amphetamines
    d. alcohol

19. During a _____ high, judgment is moderately impaired, problem solving becomes less focused and efficient, and attention is more difficult to direct; some people also report paranoia or panic symptoms.

    a. marijuana
    b. PCP
    c. Xanax
    d. cocaine

20. In _____, the soul is believed to be entered by another person or supernatural being.

    a. meditation
    b. REM sleep
    c. possession trances
    d. an LSD high

ANSWERS

FILL-IN EXERCISES

1. monitors; controls (or regulates)   2. attention   3. selective inattention   4. dichotic listening
5. conscious   6. repressed   7. cognitive unconscious   8. working   9. preconscious   10. split
11. 6.5; 8.5   12. circadian   13. adenosine   14. three; four   15. paradoxical   16. manifest; latent
17. meditation   18. significant; outlaw   19. psychoactive substances   20. physiologically; cultural
21. depressant   22. cocaine   23. lysergic acid diethylamide (LSD)

APPLICATION

1. Yes. This certainly sounds like insomnia. She should establish a regular sleep schedule, avoid activities that will produce autonomic nervous system arousal before bedtime, and if she cannot sleep, get up, rather than roll around endlessly in bed. She should get rid of the clock beside the bed!

2. No, this is not likely to help. The bed becomes a conditioned stimulus for anxiety resulting from not sleeping, which feeds the insomnia.

3. No, this is not likely to help. This will increase autonomic nervous system arousal and may aggravate the problem.

4. This could aggravate the problem. She might become dependent on them or her brain may develop a tolerance, requiring higher doses.

SAMPLE TEST QUESTIONS

1.	a	11.	d
2.	c	12.	a
3.	d	13.	a
4.	c	14.	c
5.	b	15.	b
6.	a	16.	d
7.	d	17.	b
8.	c	18.	d
9.	b	19.	a
10.	b	20.	c

Chapter 10
Motivation and Emotion

PART ONE: PRE-READ AND WORK
Outline and Learning Objectives

Pre-read this chapter's table of contents and end-of-chapter summary. Then, use the outline segment-by-segment to help you work through the chapter. Jot down your own questions, comments, and notes in the space provided. Make a note of difficult areas that you will need to review (include page numbers). Then, answer the questions in the learning objectives section that follows. Check off those you are confident that you can answer well. Re-read the material in the text for the questions about which you are less confident. Record the important points from your reading in the space below each question.

OUTLINE

Perspectives on Motivation

Psychodynamic Perspective

Behaviorist Perspective

Cognitive Perspective

Evolutionary Perspective

Applying the Perspectives on Motivation

172   *Chapter 10*

A Global Vista: Cultural Influences on Motivation

Eating

Homeostasis

What Turns Hunger On?

What Turns Hunger Off?

Obesity

Sexual Motivation

The Sexual Response Cycle

Sexual Orientation

From Brain to Behavior: The Biology of Homosexuality

Psychosocial Motives

Needs for Relatedness

Achievement and Other Agency Motives

The Nature and Causes of Human Motives

Emotion

Physiological Components

Subjective Experience

Emotional Expression

A Taxonomy of Emotions

From Brain to Behavior: The Neuropsychology of Emotion

Emotion Regulation

Perspectives on Emotion

LEARNING OBJECTIVES

Upon completion of Chapter 10, you should be able to answer the following questions.

1.   What two basic drives, according to Freud, motivate human behavior?

2.   How do current psychodynamic views of motivation differ from Freud's view?

3.   How do implicit motives and explicit motives differ? How do psychologists assess implicit motives?

4.   How do secondary drives differ from primary drives, and how are they acquired, according to the behaviorist perspective?

5.   Outline the conditions necessary for maximum job performance, according to goal-setting theory.

6.   What are three innate needs suggested by self-determination theory? How does this theory view the effects of reward?

7.   What are Maslow's five categories of needs? How are they organized?

8.   Describe the three levels of needs that form the basis of ERG theory.

9.   How does the theory of inclusive fitness account for the motivation to care for close relatives?

10.   What are pheromones? What role do they play in communication between organisms?

11.   Can culture shape motivation? How?

12.   What are the two phases of metabolism?

13.   In what ways can the system that regulates food intake be considered a homeostatic system?

14.   What causes us to feel like eating?

15.   What causes us to feel full?

16.   How is the experience of being overweight influenced by gender and culture?

17.   Outline the four phases of the sexual response cycle.

18.   Explain the organizational effects and activating effects of sex hormones on the nervous system and behavior. What insight do androgen insensitivity syndrome and congenital adrenal hyperplasia provide into the organizational role of sex hormones?

19.   Describe the research suggesting a biological basis for homosexuality.

20.   Why are needs for relatedness -- such as attachment, intimacy, and affiliation -- important?

21.   How do people with a high need for achievement characteristically behave?

22.   How do performance goals and mastery goals differ?

23.   How is need for achievement related to both parental and cultural expectations?

24.   What are the differences in how the James-Lange theory and the Cannon-Bard theory account for emotional experiences?

25.   Does emotional disclosure affect health? How?

26.   Can facial expressions actually influence a person's emotional state? How?

27.   What are the six facial expressions recognized by people of most cultures?

28.   What are *display rules* and how are they culturally relevant?

29.   What are the differences in how men and women experience and express emotion?

30.   How are positive and negative affect related to approach and avoidance?

31. Describe a hierarchical system for classifying emotions.

32. What are the roles of the hypothalamus, limbic system, and cortex in emotion?

33. What are the physiological mechanisms underlying two stages of emotional reaction in humans?

34. What is meant by *emotion regulation*? What are some common emotion regulation strategies that people use?

35. What have researchers found concerning the influence of unconscious emotional processes?

36. According to the Schachter-Singer theory of emotion, how do physiological arousal and cognitive interpretation interact?

37. What role does appraisal play in people's emotional responding?

38. Can mood influence the encoding and retrieval of information? How?

39. What differences exist between males and females in terms of jealousy, according to the evolutionary perspective?

PART TWO: REVIEW AND LEARN
Key Terms, Fill-In Exercises, Application and Using What You Have Learned

Before doing the exercises below, review the information you learned in this chapter. Reread the work you did in part one of this study guide chapter, plus the interim summaries and end-of-chapter summary in your textbook. Review any problem areas. Once you feel comfortable with the material, do the following exercises without referring to your notes or textbook. If you have difficulty with a term or question, mark it and come back to it. When you have finished an exercise, go back to your notes and the textbook to find the answers to the questions that gave you difficulty. Finally, check your answers (key terms against the textbook and the rest against the answer key).

KEY TERMS

Upon completion of Chapter 10, you should be able to define the following terms.

Motivation _____

_____

Drives _____

_____

Thematic Apperception Test (TAT) _____

_____

Drive reduction theorists _____

_____

Primary drive _____

_____

Secondary drive_____

_____

Incentive _____

_____

Goals _____

_____

Goal-setting theory _____

_____

Intrinsic motivation _____

_____

Self-determination theory _____

_____

Implicit motives _____

_____

Hierarchy of needs _____

_____

Self-actualization needs _____

_____

ERG theory _____

_____

Instincts _____

_____

Metabolism _____

_____

Absorptive phase _____

_____

Fasting phase _____

_____

Homeostasis _____

_____

Set point _____

_____

Feedback mechanisms _____

_____

Corrective mechanisms _____

_____

Satiety mechanisms _____

_____

Obesity _____

_____

Sexual response cycle _____

_____

Organizational effects _____

_____

Androgen insensitivity syndrome _____

_____

Congenital adrenal hyperplasia _____

_____

Activational effects _____

_____

Sexual orientation _____

_____

Psychosocial needs _____

_____

Relatedness _____

_____

Agency _____

_____

Attachment motivation _____

_____

Intimacy _____

_____

Affiliation _____

_____

Need for achievement _____

_____

Performance goals _____

_____

Performance-approach goals   _____

_____

Performance-avoidance goals   _____

_____

Mastery goals   _____

_____

Emotion (or affect)   _____

_____

James-Lange theory   _____

_____

Cannon-Bard theory   _____

_____

Emotional expression   _____

_____

Display rules   _____

_____

Basic emotions   _____

_____

Positive affect   _____

_____

Negative affect   _____

_____

Emotion regulation (or affect regulation) _____

_____

Moods _____

_____

Attributions _____

_____

Schachter-Singer theory _____

_____

FILL-IN EXERCISES

Fill in the word or words that best fit in the spaces below.

1. Motivation has two components: _____ people want to do (the goals they pursue) and _____ they want to do it.

2. Freud proposed that the two basic drives underlying human behavior are _____ and _____. Contemporary psychodynamic theorists, however, emphasize two other motives: the need for _____ to others and the need for _____-_____.

3. Many contemporary psychodynamic theorists have moved away from Freud's abstract notion of "drives" to two concepts that seem closer to the data of clinical observation: _____ and _____ .

4. The Thematic Apperception Test (TAT) taps _____ motives, whereas self-reports reflect _____ motives.

5. According to the behaviorist perspective, a _____ drive is an innate drive such as hunger, thirst, and sex. On the other hand, a _____ drive is a drive learned through conditioning and other learning mechanisms such as modeling.

6. Cognitive approaches to motivation often focus on _____ --desired outcomes established through social learning -- as a motivational construct.

7. A cognitive theory of motivation used widely by organizational psychologists interested in worker motivation is goal-_____ theory.

8. Self-determination theory suggests that people have three innate needs -- _____, _____, and relatedness to others.

9. Abraham Maslow proposed that needs are organized according to a _____.

10. _____ needs represent the most basic level of needs, according to Maslow.

11. ERG theory condenses the needs described by Maslow to the following three levels: _____, _____, and _____.

12. _____ are relatively fixed patterns of behavior that animals produce without learning.

13. Erich Fromm argued that a culture's socioeconomic system shapes people's motivations so that they _____ to act in ways that the system _____ them to act.

14. _____ refers to the body's tendency to maintain a relatively constant state that permits cells to live and function.

15. Like other homeostatic systems, the system regulating food intake includes several features. First, it has a _____ _____, a biologically optimal level that it strives to maintain. Second, it must have _____ mechanisms that provide it with information regarding the state of the system. Finally, it must have _____ mechanisms to restore it to its biologically optimal level when needed.

16. During the _____ phase of the sexual response cycle, the person's physiological and 6sychological functioning gradually returns to normal.

17. Sex hormones exert both _____ and _____ effects on the nervous system and behavior.

18. Sexual _____ refers to the direction of a person's enduring sexual attraction.

19. In contemporary Western society, approximately _____ to _____ % of men and _____ % of women consider themselves homosexual.

20. Two major clusters of psychosocial goals pursued cross-culturally are _____ (motives for connectedness with others) and _____ (motives for achievement, autonomy, mastery, power, and other self-oriented goals).

21. The need for _____ -- to do well, to succeed, and to avoid failure -- is the _____ (*best/least*) researched psychosocial motive.

22. Some people are more motivated to attain a goal (performance-_____ goals), whereas others are more motivated by the fear of not attaining it (performance-_____ goals).

23. William James's approach to emotion is also called the _____ theory of emotion.

24.   According to the _____-_____ theory, emotion-inducing stimuli simultaneously elicit both an emotional experience and bodily responses.

25.   Patterns of emotional expression considered appropriate within a culture or subculture are referred to as _____ _____.

26.   Evidence suggests that _____ *(men/women)* are able to read emotions from other people's faces and nonverbal cues better than _____ *(men/women)*.

27.   Psychologists have attempted to produce a list of _____ emotions – emotions common to the humans species, with characteristic physiological, subjective, and expressive components.

28.   Approach-oriented feelings and motives are processed to a greater extent in the _____ *(right/left)* frontal cortex, whereas avoidance-oriented feelings and motives are associated with the _____ *(right/left)* frontal cortex.

29.   Electrical stimulation of the _____ can produce attack, defense, or flight reactions, with corresponding emotions of rage or terror.

30.   The right and left hemispheres of the cortex appear to be specialized, with the _____ hemisphere dominant in processing emotional cues from others and producing facial displays of emotion.

31.   The term _____ refers to relatively enduring emotional states that can provide a background sense of positive or negative well-being.

32.   According to the _____-_____ theory, emotion involves two factors: physiological arousal and cognitive interpretation. Research shows, however, that while _____ may intensify emotional experience, it may not be necessary for an emotion to occur.

33.   According to Robert Zajonc, people become more positive about a stimulus the more times it is displayed to them, a phenomenon referred to as the *mere* _____ *effect*.

USING WHAT YOU HAVE LEARNED

For some time, it has been known that cigarette smoking is linked to a host of serious medical problems, including increased risk of cardiac problems, emphysema, circulatory problems, and especially lung cancer. The risks inherent in smoking are well-publicized. There are anti-smoking ads on TV and in other media. As well, speakers address teenagers in high school, exhorting them not to begin smoking or, if they already have, to quit smoking. The percentage of the population that smokes has declined significantly. Yet many teenagers still take up smoking.

A national committee has been formed to investigate the causes of teenage smoking. You have been appointed to the committee, because it is well known that you are able to understand motivation from multiple perspectives. The committee turns to you for a brief report on what might underlie the apparently self-destructive behavior of teenagers who take up smoking. They want to attack this problem from as many angles as possible and ask you to "cover all the bases," theoretically. Referring to as many perspectives as possible, how would you explain people continuing to smoke, despite the risk? What suggestions would you offer to deal with this problem?

APPLICATION

Situation

Two students in your psychology class are having a heated debate about how thinking and feeling are related. One argues that how she feels affects what she thinks. She says that when she's feeling down, everything looks negative, while on days when she's feeling really happy, she can hardly even remember negative things. The other student agrees that thinking and feeling are related, but argues that it's thinking that affects feeling, and not the other way around. She argues that it's how her friend interprets the situation that leads to feeling down or really happy. Who's right?

Questions to Answer

1. With reference to the various perspectives on emotion covered in the chapter, discuss how emotion and cognition are related.

2. Try for yourself to see how cognition and emotion are related. Pay attention to your thoughts and attributions when your mood changes. Does your mood affect your thoughts? Can you influence your emotional state by changing the content of your cognitions?

3. What role might the physiological components of emotion play in the relation between emotion and cognition?

4. What role does cognition play in people's emotional reaction to stressful situations? Is there a role for cognition in the coping process?

PART THREE: TEST AND KNOW
SAMPLE TEST QUESTIONS

Test how well you have learned this chapter's material by answering the sample test questions. You may wish to mark your answers on a separate sheet of paper so you can reuse this test for exam review. Once you have completed the exam, check your answers and then go back to your notes and the textbook to review questions you found difficult.

1.   Which of the following can be considered a secondary drive?

    a.   the desire for food   b.   the desire for water
    c.   the desire for money   d.   the desire for sex

2.   Self-determination theory suggests that people have three innate needs:

    a.   existence, belongingness, goals
    b.   physiological needs, safety needs, belongingness needs
    c.   attachment, sex, aggression
    d.   competence, autonomy, relatedness to others

3.   Self-actualization needs differ from other needs in Maslow's hierarchy in that they are

    a.   deficiency needs   b.   growth needs
    c.   belongingness needs   d.   esteem needs

4.   ERG theory condenses Maslow's hierarchy to three levels:

    a.   esteem, relatedness, growth   b.   existence, reproduction, growth
    c.   existence, resolution, growth   d.   existence, relatedness, growth

5.   The absorptive phase and fasting phase are the two phases of

    a.   the sexual response cycle   b.   homeostasis
    c.   metabolism   d.   palatability

6.   Mechanisms for "turning off" ingestive behavior are known as

    a.   satiety mechanisms   b.   corrective mechanisms
    c.   feedback mechanisms   d.   set point mechanisms

7.   Maximum arousal occurs during which phase of the sexual response cycle?

    a.   resolution   b.   plateau
    c.   orgasm   d.   excitement

8.   A disorder in which the adrenal glands secrete too much androgen in utero, masculinizing the genitals in females, is

    a.   congenital adrenal hyperplasia   b.   androgen insensitivity syndrome
    c.   maternal stress syndrome   d.   anorexia nervosa

9.   The direction of a person's enduring sexual attraction is referred to as

    a.   sexual preference   b.   sexual response
    c.   sexual orientation   d.   sexual motivation

10.   The desire for physical and psychological proximity to another person is called

    a.   the excitement phase of the sexual response cycle
    b.   attachment motivation
    c.   sexual attraction
    d.   affiliation motivation

11.   Women who report having _____ are 10 times less likely to suffer depression following a stressful event than women who do not.

    a.   a confidante   b.   an active sexual life
    c.   a rewarding career   d.   money

12.   People high in need for achievement

    a.   enjoy being challenged and are not worried about failing
    b.   worry so much about failure that they will only undertake tasks if they are assured of success
    c.   tend to take risks because of their insatiable need for challenge
    d.   enjoy being challenged but do not want to fail

13.   Bill is studying photography. He's not doing it to get the diploma that comes at the end of his program. Rather, his primary purpose is to become a better photographer. His goal would be described as a

    a.   performance goal   b.   mastery goal
    c.   mastery-avoidance goal   d.   performance-avoidance goal

14.   The James-Lange theory of emotion sees the origins of emotion in

    a.   the peripheral nervous system
    b.   the cognitive appraisal of situation
    c.   the attributions people make concerning their ability to cope
    d.   how we encode and retrieve information about an experience

15.   In addition to indicating a person's emotional state, facial expressions

     a.   provide insight into his or her implicit motivation
     b.   tell you what he or she is thinking
     c.   can indicate phases of the sexual response cycle
     d.   can influence patterns of autonomic response

16.   Cross cultural studies have identified six facial expressions recognized by people of all cultures. These are

     a.   surprise, fear, anger, disgust, happiness, sadness
     b.   anger, fear, curiosity, sadness, contempt, love
     c.   fear, trust, anticipation, love, hate, curiosity
     d.   guilt, shame, fear, anger, joy, friendliness

17.   Positive and negative affect are regulated by different neurotransmitter systems. For example, people who are "fear driven" are hypothesized to have an abundance of or greater reaction to

     a.   dopamine   b.   serotonin
     c.   norepinephrine   d.   endorphins

18.   Probably the most important limbic structure for emotion is the

     a.   hypothalamus   b.   cerebellum
     c.   thalamus   d.   amygdala

19.   The notion that a cognitive judgment or attribution is crucial to emotional experience is central to which theory of emotions?

     a.   James-Lange   b.   Schachter-Singer
     c.   Cannon-Bard   d.   Robert Zajonc's

20.   The finding that people more readily recall positive information when in a positive mood illustrates that

     a.   positive information is much easier to encode than negative information
     b.   negative information is much harder to recall than positive information
     c.   emotional states influence both encoding and recall of information in memory
     d.   both a and b

ANSWERS

FILL-IN EXERCISES

1. what; how strongly   2. sex, aggression; relatedness, self-esteem   3. wishes; fears   4. implicit (unconscious); explicit (conscious)   5. primary, secondary   6. goals   7. setting   8. competence, autonomy   9. hierarchy   10. physiological   11. existence, relatedness, growth   12. instincts   13. want; needs   14. homeostasis   15. set point; feedback; corrective   16. resolution   17. organizational; activational   18. orientation   19. 2%; 7%; 1%   20. relatedness; agency   21. achievement; best   22. approach; avoidance   23. peripheral   24 Cannon-Bard   25. display rules   26. women; men   27. basic   28. left; right   29. hypothalamus   30. right   31. mood   32. Schachter-Singer; arousal   33. exposure

SAMPLE TEST QUESTIONS

1.	c	11.	a
2.	d	12.	d
3.	b	13.	b
4.	d	14.	a
5.	c	15.	d
6.	a	16.	a
7.	b	17.	c
8.	a	18.	d
9.	c	19.	b
10.	b	20.	c

Chapter 11
Health, Stress, and Coping

PART ONE: PRE-READ AND WORK
Outline and Learning Objectives

Pre-read this chapter's table of contents and end-of-chapter summary. Then, use the outline segment-by-segment to help you work through the chapter. Jot down your own questions, comments, and notes in the space provided. Make a note of difficult areas that you will need to review (include page numbers). Then, answer the questions in the learning objectives section that follows. Check off those you are confident that you can answer well. Re-read the material in the text for the questions about which you are less confident. Record the important points from your reading in the space below each question.

OUTLINE

Health Psychology

History of Health Psychology

Theories of Health Behavior

Health-Compromising Behaviors

One Step Further: Self-Presentation and Health

Barriers to Health Promotion

Stress

Stress as a Psychobiological Process

Stress as a Transactional Process

Sources of Stress

Stress and Health

Coping

Coping Mechanisms

A Global Vista: The Impact of Culture on Coping Styles

Social Support

One Step Further: Disclosure and Health

The Future of Health Psychology

LEARNING OBJECTIVES

Upon completion of Chapter 11, you should be able to answer the following questions.

1.   What is health psychology?

2.   Discuss the different historical views of the roles of body, mind, and spiritual forces as contributors to disease.

3.   Describe the key elements of each of the following theories of health behavior:

Health Belief Model

Protection Motivation Theory of Health

Theory of Reasoned Action

Theory of Planned Behavior

4.   How is obesity defined?

5.   What are the physical and psychological consequences of obesity?

6.   How do genes and environmental factors contribute to obesity?

7.   What are the pros and cons of dieting, appetite-suppressing drugs, and surgery for the treatment of obesity?

8.   What are the consequences of smoking?

9.   How do genes and environmental factors contribute to smoking?

10.   Briefly discuss the major methods of treating smoking.

11.   How does self-presentation contribute to engaging in risky behaviors in the following areas:

condom use

suntanning

smoking, alcohol, and illegal drugs

exercise

accidents and injuries

12.   How are alcoholism and problem drinking defined?

13.   How do genes and environmental factors contribute to alcoholism?

14.   What are the major consequences of alcoholism?

15.   Briefly describe some major ways of treating alcoholism.

16.   What roles can health psychologists play in the prevention of sexually transmitted diseases such as HIV/AIDS?

17.   Discuss each of the following barriers to health promotion:

Individual barriers

Family barriers

Health system barriers

Community, cultural, and ethnic barriers

18.   In what ways can stress be considered both a psychobiological and a transactional process?

19.   What are the three stages of the general adaptation syndrome?

20.   What are the differences between primary appraisal and secondary appraisal according to Richard Lazarus's model of stress and coping?

21.   How are life events, catastrophes, and daily hassles sources of stress? What are the possible effects of each?

22.   How does stress affect the body's capacity to fight illness?

23.   What is the Type-A behavior pattern? How is it related to health problems?

24.   Is optimism/pessimism related to health? How?

25.   How do problem-focused strategies for coping with stress differ from emotion-focused strategies?

26.   Explain the differences between low-effort syndrome and John Henryism.

27.   What are two explanations for the beneficial effects of social support in coping with stress?

28.   How does emotional disclosure affect health?

PART TWO: REVIEW AND LEARN
Key Terms, Fill-In Exercises, Application and Using What You Have Learned

Before doing the exercises below, review the information you learned in this chapter. Reread the work you did in part one of this study guide chapter, plus the interim summaries and end-of-chapter summary in your textbook. Review any problem areas. Once you feel comfortable with the material, do the following exercises without referring to your notes or textbook. If you have difficulty with a term or question, mark it and come back to it. When you have finished an exercise, go back to your notes and the textbook to find the answers to the questions that gave you difficulty. Finally, check your answers (key terms against the textbook and the rest against the answer key).

KEY TERMS

Upon completion of Chapter 11, you should be able to define the following terms.

Health psychology   _____

_____

Trephination   _____

_____

Humoral theory of illness   _____

_____

Cartesian dualism _____

_____

Cellular theory of illness _____

_____

Biomedical model _____

_____

Psychosomatic medicine _____

_____

Biopsychosocial model _____

_____

Health belief model _____

_____

Perceived susceptibility _____

_____

Optimistic bias _____

_____

Perceived seriousness (or severity) _____

_____

Benefits _____

_____

Barriers _____

_____

Cues to action _____

_____

Protection motivation theory of health _____

_____

Self-efficacy _____

_____

Theory of reasoned action _____

_____

Attitudes _____

_____

Subjective norms _____

_____

Theory of planned behavior _____

_____

Body mass index (BMI) _____

_____

Obesity _____

_____

Overweight _____

_____

Set point _____

_____

Susceptible gene hypothesis _____

_____

Self presentation _____

_____

Alcoholism _____

_____

Problem drinkers _____

_____

Self-handicapping _____

_____

Spontaneous remission _____

_____

Detoxification _____

_____

Aversion therapy _____

_____

Stress _____

_____

General adaptation syndrome _____

_____

Primary appraisal _____

_____

Secondary appraisal _____

_____

Emotional forecasting _____

_____

Stressors _____

_____

Acculturative stress _____

_____

Catastrophes _____

_____

Daily hassles _____

_____

Psychoneuroimmunology _____

_____

Immune system _____

_____

Antibodies _____

_____

Type A behavior pattern _____

_____

Coping _____

_____

Low effort syndrome   _____

_____

John Henryism   _____

_____

Social support   _____

_____

FILL-IN EXERCISES

Fill in the word or words that best fit in the spaces below.

1.   _____ was an ancient practice that involved drilling holes in the skulls of diseased individuals to allow evil spirits to escape.

2.   Hippocrates proposed the _____ theory of illness which asserts that disease is caused by an imbalance in the four fluids of the body.

3.   Descartes's theory of Cartesian dualism contends that the _____ and the _____ are completely separate entities.

4.   The field of _____ medicine holds that changes in physiology mediate the relationship between unconscious conflicts and illness.

5.   According to the _____ model, health and illness stem from a combination of biological, psychological, and social factors.

6.   One of the earliest theories of health behavior was the _____ _____ model, which suggests that health behaviors are predicted by four factors: perceived susceptibility; perceived seriousness, benefits and barriers, and cues to action.

7.   Many people experience a(n) _____ bias, by which they believe that they are far less likely than other people to contract particular illnesses.

8.   In deciding whether or not to adopt a health behavior, people evaluate whether the _____ to be gained by stopping outweigh the _____ associated with the termination of the behavior.

9.   According to the theory of reasoned action, behavioral intentions are a function of two components: _____ toward the behavior and the subjective _____ surrounding the behavior.

10.   Obesity refers to an excessive accumulation of body fat, in excess of _____ percent in women and _____ percent in men.

11.   _____, or stomach stapling, is a treatment for obesity used with some individuals who are at least _____ percent overweight.

12.   Self-_____ refers to people's attempts to control the impressions that others form of them.

13.   A person is identified as having _____ when he or she is physiologically dependent on alcohol.

14.   Some people quit drinking or greatly reduce their alcohol intake on their own, without any formal method of intervention, a process called _____ _____.

15.   The first stage of alcohol rehabilitation is _____, or the process of drying out.

16.   Antabuse is a drug used as a means of discouraging problem drinking, in a treatment known as _____ therapy

17.   The organism is especially vulnerable to illness in the _____ stage of the general adaptation syndrome.

18.   According to Lazarus's model of stress and coping, in the _____ appraisal stage, the person decides whether the situation is benign, stressful, or irrelevant.

19.   Change is one of the most significant sources of _____.

20.   _____ stress refers to the stress that people experience when trying to adapt to a new culture.

21.   Stressors of massive proportion are referred to as _____.

22.   _____ _____ are minor annoyances of everyday life that contribute to stress.

23.   _____ examines the influence of psychosocial factors on the functioning of the immune system.

24.   In the immune system, B cells produce _____, protein molecules that attach themselves to foreign invaders and mark them for destruction.

25.   Individuals who are impatient, hard-driving, ambitious, competitive, and hostile display what is called the _____ behavior pattern.

26.   Coping mechanisms aimed at changed the stressful situation are called _____-focused. Efforts to alter one's thoughts about the situation, or to alter the unpleasant affective consequences of stress, are called _____-focused.

27. _____ syndrome describes the tendency to exert minimal effort to escape stressful social and economic circumstances.

USING WHAT YOU HAVE LEARNED

How's Your Stress?

One of the sources of stress you read about in Chapter 11 was life events. Consider the stressful life events you have confronted over the past 12 months. Have you experienced any major stressors? Have you had to deal with more than one stressful life event? Can you see how their effects can add up?

How many of the stressors you're dealing with can be considered "challenges," that is, positive changes in your life? Can you see how even positive life events can be considered stressors?

What are some of the "daily hassles" you deal with? Is it apparent to you how they can be considered sources of stress?

How do you deal with stress? Do you use physical exercise or relaxation? How about social support? Are you able to talk to another person or people about the life events you're dealing with?

What would you say are the most common stressors that university students have to cope with?

APPLICATION

Situation

Two of your friends are engaged in a heated discussion about obesity. One argues that obesity is the biggest preventable health problem after smoking. She believes that obese people need to use only a little self-control and reduce their calorie intake to control their weight problem. The other student agrees and adds that, as far as she's concerned, the "majority" of women are overweight. The two students agree and go on to talk about how "lazy," unattractive, and socially inept overweight people are.

Having just studied the topic of motivation, you feel you are in a position to offer some informed input. Based on what you have read, address the following points.

Questions to Answer

1. To what extent is obesity a health problem?

2. Is it true that the majority of women are overweight? What is the medical definition of obesity? Approximately what proportion of the adult American population is obese?

3. How would you respond to the students' statements about the laziness, attractiveness, and social skills of overweight people?

4. Is it true that all that's needed is willpower and dieting? How could you explain to these students that the issue is more complicated than they think.

PART THREE: TEST AND KNOW
SAMPLE TEST QUESTIONS

Test how well you have learned this chapter's material by answering the sample test questions. You may wish to mark your answers on a separate sheet of paper so you can reuse this test for exam review. Once you have completed the exam, check your answers and then go back to your notes and the textbook to review questions you found difficult.

1.   Hippocrates proposed the humoral theory of illness which asserts that disease is caused by an imbalance in the four fluids of the body. Which of the following is **NOT** one of these four fluids?

    a.   yellow saliva   b.   blood
    c.   phlegm   d.   black bile

2.   According to Cartesian dualism

    a.   mind and body cannot be separated
    b.   the spirit exists independently of the mind
    c.   body and soul are fused
    d.   mind and body are separate entities

3.   Ancillary factors that determine whether or not a person is willing to begin a healthy behavior or terminate an unhealthy one are referred to as

    a.   side effects
    b.   threats
    c.   cues to action
    d.   planned behaviors

4.   According to the Protection Motivation Theory of Health,

    a.   attitudes and subjective norms are key elements in health behavior
    b.   self-efficacy is a key element in health behavior
    c.   many people experience an optimistic bias leading them to believe they are less likely than others to contract particular illnesses.
    d.   all of the above

5.   Obesity is typically measured in terms of

    a.   total weight
    b.   waist circumference
    c.   body mass index
    d.   set point index

6.   What proportion of American children aged 6 to 11 is overweight?

    a.   5%
    b.   15%
    c.   25%
    d.   50%

7.   The hormone _____ is produced by fat tissue and operates on the hypothalamus to regulate body weight.

    a.   adrenalin
    b.   estrogen
    c.   cortisol
    d.   leptin

8   Compared to slow nicotine metabolizers, fast metabolizers

    a.   are less likely to experience the negative effects of smoking
    b.   are more susceptible to treatment
    c.   are more likely to experience smoking as aversive
    d.   are less likely to smoke

9   Approximately what percent of people who attempt to quit smoking remain smoke free?

    a.   15%
    b.   25%
    c.   50%
    d.   65%

10   The best known treatment for alcoholism is

    a.   aversion therapy
    b.   hypnosis
    c.   alcoholics anonymous
    d.   detoxification

11.   Which of the following is true concerning STDs?

    a.   Women are at greater risk for contracting a sexually transmitted disease than men.
    b.   The consequences of contracting a sexually transmitted disease tend to be more serious for men than for women.
    c.   The tendency to contract a sexually transmitted disease appears to have a strong genetic component.
    d.   all of the above

12.   The three stages of the general adaptation syndrome, by which the body reacts to stress, include

    a.   alarm, appraisal, coping
    b.   alarm, fleeing, fighting
    c.   alarm, plateau, recovery
    d.   alarm, resistance, exhaustion

13.   During the alarm stage of the general adaptation syndrome

    a.   the organism is especially vulnerable to illness
    b.   the body eventually wears down, if the phase lasts long enough
    c.   adrenalin and other hormones are released and the sympathetic nervous system is
          activated
    d.   all systems may appear to have returned to normal, although the body continues to use its
          resources at an accelerated rate

14.   According to Richard Lazarus, stress and coping involve two stages. The stage in which a person
       evaluates his or her options and determines how to respond is referred to as the

    a.   coping stage
    b.   resistance stage
    c.   primary appraisal stage
    d.   secondary appraisal stage

15.   Richard Lazarus distinguishes three types of stress:

    a.   challenge, threat, catastrophes
    b.   exhaustion, harm or loss, catastrophes
    c.   harm or loss, threat, challenge
    d.   hassles, catastrophes, life events

16.   The most stressful of life events, according to the Holmes-Rahe Life Events Rating Scale is

    a.   being fired at work
    b.   death of a spouse
    c.   divorce
    d.   being jailed

17.   Daily hassles

    a.   in contrast to life events are unlikely to serve as stressors
    b.   can easily be coped with by using a little denial
    c.   are stressful only for individuals displaying the Type-A behavior pattern
    d.   are often central to the subjective experience of stress

18.   The Type-A characteristic that is particularly related to heart disease is

        a.   hostility
        b.   competitiveness
        c.   impatience
        d.   ambitiousness

19.   John Henryism is a coping style characterized by

        a.   a tendency to work hard and cope actively despite difficult circumstances
        b.   the tendency to exert minimal effort to escape stressful social and economic circumstances
        c.   impatience, ambition, competitiveness, and a "hard-driving" approach to life
        d.   the tendency to explain bad events in negative, self-blaming ways

20.   Social support is an effective resource for coping with stress and involves

        a.   being cared for by the state until the person is able to cope on his or her own again
        b.   the presence of others that one can confide in and from whom one can expect help and concern
        c.   financial resources provided by social service agencies for people experiencing catastrophic stress
        d.   both a and c

ANSWERS

FILL-IN EXERCISES

1. trephination   2. humoral   3. mind; body   4. psychosomatic   5. biopsychosocial   6. health belief
7. optimistic   8. benefits; barriers   9. attitudes; norms   10. 30; 20   11. gastroplasty; 100   12. presentation
13. alcoholism   14. spontaneous remission   15. detoxification   16. aversion   17. resistance
18. primary   19. stress   20. acculturative   21. catastrophes   22. daily hassles
23. psychoneuroimmunology   24. antibodies   25. Type A   26. problem; emotion   27. low-effort

APPLICATION

1.   Although tobacco is still the primary health threat, obesity ranks a close second. Obesity is associated with heart disease, high blood pressure, diabetes, gallstones, sleep apneas, and some cancers and an increased mortality rate.

2.   Over half of all adult Americans are overweight or obese, with more women than men being classified as both overweight and obese. Obesity refers to an excessive accumulation of body fat, in excess of 30% in women and 20% in men. People are identified as being overweight if the have a body mass index between 25% and 30% depending on their gender and age.

3.   These are stereotypes that can lead to differences in how obese people are treated, which can result lowered self-esteem and negative expectations about how others will treat you .People who are obese often experience psychological difficulties stemming from the stigma attached to obesity and the subsequent discrimination experienced by obese individuals.

4.   It's not as simple as just willpower and dieting -- genetic, social, and psychological factors may all contribute to obesity. Genetic factors may account for up to 40% of the etiology of obesity. Because some people are resistant to the hormone leptin, they are unable to effectively control their weight around their set point. Low self-esteem, anxiety, and depression may also be implicated in obesity.

SAMPLE TEST QUESTIONS

1.	a	11.	a
2.	d	12.	d
3.	c	13.	c
4.	b	14.	d
5.	c	15.	c
6.	b	16.	b
7.	d	17.	d
8.	a	18.	a
9.	b	19.	a
10.	c	20.	b

Chapter 12
Personality

PART ONE: PRE-READ AND WORK
Outline and Learning Objectives

Pre-read this chapter's table of contents and end-of-chapter summary. Then, use the outline segment-by-segment to help you work through the chapter. Jot down your own questions, comments, and notes in the space provided. Make a note of difficult areas that you will need to review (include page numbers). Then, answer the questions in the learning objectives section that follows. Check off those you are confident that you can answer well. Re-read the material in the text for the questions about which you are less confident. Record the important points from your reading in the space below each question.

OUTLINE

Psychodynamic Theories

Freud's Models

Object Relations Theories

One Step Further: Assessing Unconscious Patterns

Contributions and Limitations of Psychodynamic Theories

Cognitive Social Theories

Encoding and Personal Relevance

Expectancies and Competences

Self-Regulation

Contributions and Limitations of Cognitive-Social Theories

From Brain to Behavior: Driving Mr. Albert

Trait Theories

Eysenck's Theory

The Five Factor Model

Is Personality Consistent?

Contributions and Limitations of Trait Theories

Humanistic Theories

Rogers's Person-Centered Approach

Existential Approaches to Personality

Contributions and Limitations of Humanistic Theories

Genetics and Personality

Personality and Culture

Linking Personality and Culture

A Global Vista: Interactionist Approaches to Personality and Culture

LEARNING OBJECTIVES

Upon completion of Chapter 12, you should be able to answer the following questions.

1. Identify and describe the three types of mental processes comprising Freud's topographical model.

2. What role do ambivalence and conflict play in an individual's actions?

3.   What are the major characteristics of each of the following psychosexual stages?

Oral stage

Anal stage

Phallic stage

Latency stage

Genital stage

4.   How is identification linked to the Oedipus complex?

5.   What are the similarities and differences between girls and boys in terms of the Oedipus complex?

6.   Compare the roles of the id, ego, and superego.

7.   Identify seven defense mechanisms and describe how each functions.

8.   What is the focus of object relations theories and how do these approaches differ from Freudian theory?

9.   What are the major methods used by psychodynamic psychologists to assess unconscious patterns?

10.   What are the major contributions and limitations of psychodynamic theories?

11.   How do cognitive-social theories of personality differ from both behaviorist and psychodynamic views?

12. What is the importance of personal relevance in how people respond to a situation?

13. How do people's expectancies and competences influence the actions they carry out?

14. What role is played by self-regulation in the execution of behavior?

15. What is the difference, according to Eysenck's theory, between traits and types?

16. Describe the three overarching psychological types identified by Eysenck.

17. Which five superordinate personality traits make up the *Big Five* factors?

18. Explain Walter Mischel's argument that circumstances largely determine people's behavior. What are the arguments against this notion?

19. Can it be said that personality traits are consistent over time?

20. What are the limitations of trait theory approaches to personality?

21. What are the core assumptions underlying Rogers's person-centered approach to personality?

22. What do existentialists mean when they say that people, unlike other animals and physical objects, have no fixed nature and must essentially create themselves?

23.   What is death anxiety and how has it been investigated experimentally?

24.   What are the major contributions and limitations of humanistic approaches to personality?

25.   What do studies comparing MZ and DZ twins reared together and apart reveal about the heritability of various personality traits?

26.   How are personality and culture related in the following approaches?

Freud's approach

The culture pattern approach

Interactionist approaches

PART TWO: REVIEW AND LEARN
Key Terms, Fill-In Exercises, Application and Using What You Have Learned

Before doing the exercises below, review the information you learned in this chapter. Reread the work you did in part one of this study guide chapter, plus the interim summaries and end-of-chapter summary in your textbook. Review any problem areas. Once you feel comfortable with the material, do the following exercises without referring to your notes or textbook. If you have difficulty with a term or question, mark it and come back to it. When you have finished an exercise, go back to your notes and the textbook to find the answers to the questions that gave you difficulty. Finally, check your answers (key terms against the textbook and the rest against the answer key).

KEY TERMS

Upon completion of Chapter 12, you should be able to define the following terms.

Personality _____

_____

Structure of personality _____

_____

Individual differences _____

_____

Psychodynamics _____

_____

Topographic model _____

_____

Conscious mental processes _____

_____

Preconscious mental processes _____

_____

Unconscious mental processes _____

_____

Ambivalence _____

_____

Conflict _____

_____

Compromise formations _____

_____

Drive (or instinct) model _____

_____

Libido _____

_____

Psychosexual stages _____

_____

Freud's developmental model _____

_____

Oral stage _____

_____

Fixations _____

_____

Anal stage _____

_____

Regression _____

_____

Phallic stage _____

_____

Identification _____

_____

Oedipus complex _____

_____

Castration complex _____

_____

Penis envy _____

_____

Latency stage _____

_____

Genital stage _____

_____

Structural model_____

_____

Id _____

_____

Primary process thinking_____

_____

Superego _____

_____

Ego _____

_____

Secondary process thinking _____

_____

Defense mechanisms _____

_____

Repression _____

_____

Denial _____

_____

Projection _____

_____

Reaction formation _____

_____

Sublimation _____

_____

Rationalization _____

_____

Passive aggression _____

_____

Object relations _____

_____

Relational theories   _____

_____

Life history methods   _____

_____

Projective tests _____

_____

Rorschach inkblot test   _____

_____

Personal constructs   _____

_____

Personal value _____

_____

Life tasks   _____

_____

Expectancies   _____

_____

Behavior-outcome expectancy   _____

_____

Self-efficacy expectancy_____

_____

Competences _____

_____

Self-regulation _____

_____

Traits _____

_____

Extroversion _____

_____

Neuroticism _____

_____

Psychoticism _____

_____

Five Factor Model (FFM) _____

_____

Situational variables _____

_____

Principle of aggregation _____

_____

Temperament _____

_____

Person-by-environment interactions _____

_____

Humanistic approaches _____

_____

Person-centered approach   _____

_____

Phenomenal experience _____

_____

Empathy   _____

_____

True self   _____

_____

False self   _____

_____

Conditions of worth   _____

_____

Ideal self   _____

_____

Actualizing tendency   _____

_____

Existentialism _____

_____

Existential dread   _____

_____

Heritability   _____

_____

Culture pattern approach   _____

_____

Interactionist approaches   _____

_____

FILL-IN EXERCISES

Fill in the word or words that best fit in the spaces below.

1.   The _____ of personality refers to the organization of enduring patterns of thought, feeling, motivation, and behavior.

2.   The ways people vary from one another in their characteristics are referred to as _____ differences.

3.   Freud's _____ model divided mental processes into three types. _____ mental processes are rational, goal-directed thoughts at the center of awareness. _____ mental processes are not conscious, but could become conscious at any point. Finally, _____ mental processes are irrational, organized along associative lines rather than by logic.

4.   The term _____ refers to conflicting feelings or motives that affect people's behavior.

5.   The solutions people develop to maximize fulfillment of conflicting motives are referred to as _____ formations.

6.   Freud used the term _____ to refer to pleasure seeking, sensuality, and love, as well as the sexual drive.

7.   Freud proposed a theory of _____ stages – stages in the development of personality, sexuality, and motivation.

8.   _____ are conflicts or concerns that persist beyond the developmental period in which they arise.

9.   The term _____ means reverting to conflicts or modes of managing emotion characteristic of an earlier stage of development.

10. The process of _____ involves making another person part of yourself, trying to become more like the person by adopting his or her attitudes and values.

11. The _____ _____ refers to Freud's hypothesis that little boys want an exclusive relationship with their mothers, and little girls want an exclusive relationship with their fathers.

12. During the _____ stage, children repress their sexual impulses and continue to identify with their same-sex parents.

13. Freud's structural model posits three sets of mental forces or structures: _____, _____, and _____.

14. Rational, logical, and goal-directed thinking, characteristic of the ego, is referred to as _____ _____ thinking.

15. _____ is an unconscious mechanism that keeps thoughts or memories, that would be too threatening to acknowledge, from awareness.

16. _____ _____ is a defense mechanism whereby a person turns unacceptable feelings or impulses into their opposites.

17. _____ _____ theories focus on interpersonal disturbances and mental processes that underlie the capacity for relatedness to others

18. _____ _____ methods aim to understand the whole person in the context of his or her life experience and environment.

19. George Kelly coined the term personal _____ to refer to mental representations of the people, places, things, and events that are significant to a person.

20. The importance individuals attach to various outcomes or potential outcomes, according to the cognitive social approach, is referred to as _____ value.

21. According to the cognitive social approach, whether people carry out various actions depends on both expectancies and _____.

22. A commonly used method of measuring traits involves having people answer questions about themselves by filling out a _____.

23. Openness to experience, conscientiousness, extroversion, agreeableness, and neuroticism are referred to as the _____ _____ factors by trait theorists.

24. According to Walter Mischel, _____ variables – the circumstances in which people find themselves – largely determine their behavior.

25. Inhibition to the unfamiliar, a cluster of attributes in children that includes shyness and anxiety in the face of novelty, appears to be an aspect of _____, a basic personality disposition heavily influenced by genes.

26. According to Carl Rogers, individuals often wear a mask, which he refers to as a _____ self, which is the result of their natural desire to gain the _____ regard of other people.

27. Rogers proposed that the primary motivation in humans is an _____ tendency -- a desire to fulfill the full range of needs that humans experience.

28. The recognition that life has no absolute value or meaning and that ultimately we all face death is a problem referred to as existential _____.

29. _____ approaches hold that personality, culture, and economics are all interrelated – that is, causality is multidirectional.

APPLICATION

With reference to Freud's psychosexual stages, explain the behavior of each of the following individuals.

1. Brenda is an extremely insecure woman. She seems to be always concerned with what other people are thinking of her. She has a real need for the approval of others and can't seem to make any decisions on her own. She clings to people, as if she's afraid to let go in case they'll leave her.

2. Ted is really stingy. He just won't share with anybody. Not only that, he's so concerned that everything be done "just so." You might call him obsessive. Hardly anybody can work with him, because he always insists that everything be done his way.

3. Mary is the most disorganized person you've ever seen. Her room is an absolute mess. She never completes her assignments, because she always loses them. She's always late for class; in fact, she even missed an exam last term because she overslept.

4. Bill always has something in his mouth, often a cigarette. Lately, he's been trying to quit smoking by chewing bubble gum (he blows bubbles all the time and pops them, even in class). When he's not smoking or chewing gum, you'll probably find him sucking on a lollipop.

5. Steve spends all his free time in the gym, working out. He has muscles where most people don't even know there are muscles! When he's not in the gym, he's trying to impress women. It's really important to him that women are attracted to him.

USING WHAT YOU HAVE LEARNED

Identify the individual or theory most closely associated with each of the following concepts.

1. Big Five factors	10. Empathy
2. Regression	11. Self-regulation
3. Positive regard	12. Extroversion
4. Types	13. Libido
5. Self-efficacy expectancy	14. Ideal self
6. False self	15. Existential dread
7. Repertory grid technique	16. Preconscious
8. Primary process thinking	17. Personal value
9. Personal constructs	18. Competences

PART THREE: TEST AND KNOW
SAMPLE TEST QUESTIONS

Test how well you have learned this chapter's material by answering the sample test questions. You may wish to mark your answers on a separate sheet of paper so you can reuse this test for exam review. Once you have completed the exam, check your answers and then go back to your notes and the textbook to review questions you found difficult.

1.   According to Freud, preconscious mental processes are

    a.   rational, goal-directed thoughts at the center of awareness
    b.   thoughts that are not conscious, but could become conscious at any time
    c.   irrational, inaccessible thoughts
    d.   inert, unconscious thoughts

2.   Freud proposed two basic drives motivating human behavior:

    a.   sex and aggression
    b.   aggression and violence
    c.   sex and survival
    d.   aggression and destructiveness

3.   Which of Freud's stages is characterized by conflicts with parents about compliance and defiance?

        a.   oral
        b.   anal
        c.   phallic
        d.   latency

4.   Fixations at the latency stage can lead to

        a.   conflicts about giving and receiving
        b.   a preoccupation with attracting mates
        c.   exaggerated needs for approval
        d.   asexuality

5.   A fixation at the oral stage can lead to

        a.   conflicts about giving and receiving
        b.   a preoccupation with attracting mates
        c.   exaggerated needs for approval
        d.   appearing totally asexual

6.   The reservoir of sexual and aggressive energy is the

        a.   libido
        b.   ego
        c.   id
        d.   latency

7.   Secondary process thinking is characteristic of the

        a.   libido
        b.   ego
        c.   id
        d.   anima

8.   Converting sexual or aggressive impulses into socially acceptable activities involves the defense mechanism of

        a.   denial
        b.   projection
        c.   rationalization
        d.   sublimation

9.   A hard-driving businessman, who thinks his competitors, suppliers, and customers are always trying to cheat him, may in fact be the one with questionable ethics. To recognize his own greed and lack of concern for others would conflict with his conscience. So, instead, he sees these traits in others. This defense mechanism is known as

      a.   denial
      b.   reaction formation
      c.   rationalization
      d.   projection

10.   A student who plagiarizes her term paper and justifies her actions by saying that passing the course will help her earn her public policy degree and serve the community, is using the defense mechanism of _____ to justify her dishonesty.

      a.   rationalization
      b.   sublimation
      c.   denial
      d.   passive aggression

11.   Object relations theories explain difficulties people have in maintaining intimate relationships in terms of

      a.   unconscious conflicts
      b.   a natural desire to gain the positive regard of other people
      c.   maladaptive interpersonal patterns laid down in the first few years of life
      d.   the recognition that life has no absolute value or meaning and that ultimately we will all face death

12.   A therapist shows a subject a series of ambiguous drawings, most of which depict people interacting, and asks the subject to make up a story about each drawing. The assumption is that in eliminating the ambiguity, the subject will create a story that reflects her own recurring wishes, fears, and ways of experiencing relationships. This procedure is referred to as the:

      a.   repertory grid technique
      b.   Thematic Apperception Test (TAT)
      c.   Rorschach inkblot test
      d.   life-history method

13.   George Kelly and his colleagues developed the _____ to assess individuals' personal constructs indirectly.

      a.   repertory grid technique
      b.   Thematic Apperception Test (TAT)
      c.   Rorschach inkblot test
      d.   person-centered approach

14.   Self-regulation refers to

    a.   setting goals
    b.   evaluating one's performance
    c.   adjusting one's behavior to meet goals
    d.   all of the above

15.   Which of the following is *not* used to measure traits?

    a.   asking people to report on the content of their dreams
    b.   observing people's behavior over time and in different situations
    c.   asking people who know the individual well to fill out questionnaires about his or her personality
    d.   asking people themselves to fill out a self-report questionnaire

16.   Extroversion, neuroticism, and psychoticism are three psychological types identified by

    a.   Kelly
    b.   Rogers
    c.   Eysenck
    d.   Adler

17.   The Big Five factors include

    a.   extroversion, agreeableness, conscientiousness, neuroticism, and openness to experience
    b.   extroversion, neuroticism, psychoticism, conscientiousness, and openness to experience
    c.   extroversion, expectancies, competences, self-efficacy, and openness to experience
    d.   extroversion, personal values, conscientiousness, neuroticism, and ill-temperedness

18.   Which of the following is a criticism of trait theory approaches?

    a.   They overemphasize the rational side of life and underemphasize the emotional, motivational, and irrational.
    b.   They are no more sophisticated than the theories of personality held by lay people.
    c.   They have failed to develop a substantial body of testable hypotheses and research.
    d.   They are theories aimed at interpretation of behavior that has already occurred, rather than at prediction of behavior.

19.   In Carl Rogers's view, psychology should try to understand

    a.   how beliefs, rituals, and institutions shape individuals
    b.   the ways in which unconscious conflicts underlie an individual's behavior
    c.   the way people conceive of reality and experience themselves and their world
    d.   that life has no absolute value or meaning and that ultimately we all face death

20.   According to Rogers, the fundamental tool of the psychologist is

a.   the repertory grid technique
b.   empathy
c.   projective tests like the TAT and Rorschach inkblot test
d.   direct observation of an individual across many situations

ANSWERS

FILL-IN EXERCISES

1. structure 2. individual 3. topographic; conscious, preconscious, unconscious 4. ambivalence
5. compromise 6. libido 7. psychosexual 8. fixations 9. regression 10. identification 11. Oedipus
complex 12. latency 13. id, ego, superego 14. secondary process 15. repression 16. reaction
formation 17. object relations 18. life history 19. constructs 20. personal 21. competences
22. questionnaire 23. Big Five 24. situational 25. temperament 26. false; positive 27. actualizing
28. dread 29. interactionist

APPLICATION

1. oral stage fixation
2. anal stage fixation
3. anal stage fixation
4. oral stage fixation
5. phallic stage fixation

USING WHAT YOU HAVE LEARNED

1.	trait theories	10.	humanistic (Rogers)
2.	psychodynamic (Freud)	11.	cognitive social
3.	humanistic (Rogers)	12.	trait (Eysenck)
4.	trait (Eysenck)	13.	psychodynamic (Freud)
5.	cognitive social (Bandura)	14.	humanistic (Rogers)
6.	humanistic (Rogers)	15.	existential
7.	cognitive social (Kelly)	16.	psychodynamic (Freud)
8.	psychodynamic (Freud)	17.	cognitive social
9.	cognitive social (Kelly)	18.	cognitive social

SAMPLE TEST QUESTIONS

1.	b	11.	c
2.	a	12.	b
3.	b	13.	a
4.	d	14.	d
5.	c	15.	a
6.	c	16.	c
7.	b	17.	a
8.	d	18.	b
9.	d	19.	c
10.	a	20.	b

Chapter 13
Physical and Cognitive Development

PART ONE: PRE-READ AND WORK
Outline and Learning Objectives

Pre-read this chapter's table of contents and end-of-chapter summary. Then, use the outline segment-by-segment to help you work through the chapter. Jot down your own questions, comments, and notes in the space provided. Make a note of difficult areas that you will need to review (include page numbers). Then, answer the questions in the learning objectives section that follows. Check off those you are confident that you can answer well. Re-read the material in the text for the questions about which you are less confident. Record the important points from your reading in the space below each question.

OUTLINE

Nature and Nurture

The Relative Importance of Early Experience

From Brain to Behavior: The Gendered Brain

Stages or Continuous Change?

Studying Development

Cross-Sectional Studies

Longitudinal Studies

Sequential Studies

Physical Development and Its Psychological Consequences

Prenatal Development

Infancy

Childhood and Adolescence

Adulthood and Aging

A Global Vista: Menopause in a Mayan Village

Cognitive Development in Infancy, Childhood, and Adolescence

Perceptual and Cognitive Development in Infancy

Piaget's Theory of Cognitive Development

Information-Processing Approach to Cognitive Development

Integrative Theories of Cognitive Development

Cognitive Development and Change in Adulthood

Cognitive Changes Associated with Aging

Aging and "Senility"

Language Development

A Critical Period for Language Development?

What Infants Know about Language

From Babbling to Bantering

The Nature of Development

LEARNING OBJECTIVES

Upon completion of Chapter 13, you should be able to answer the following questions.

1.   What is meant by the term critical period? Why is this concept controversial when considering human development?

2.   How does continuous developmental change differ from change that occurs in stages?

3.   What are the advantages and disadvantages of three types of research design used by developmental psychologists?

4.   What are the three periods of prenatal development?

5.   What is meant by the term *teratogen*? Describe the prenatal effects of the following three teratogens: alcohol, crack cocaine, and maternal stress.

6.   What are the characteristics of puberty? Are there differences between boys and girls in the effects of early maturation?

7.   What are the major consequences of menopause? Can culture influence women's reactions to this event?

8.   What are the changes in male sexuality that begin at mid-life?

9.   What is "ageism?"

10.   What methods do researchers use to study infant perception and cognition?

11.   Describe the visual and auditory capabilities of infants.

12.   What has been found concerning intermodal understanding in infants?

13.   What has research shown concerning memory in infants?

14.   How are assimilation and accommodation involved in the process of adaptation to the environment?

15.   What are the major characteristics and the approximate age-range of each of Piaget's four stages of cognitive development?

16.   What is "object permanence?" Approximately when does this concept develop?

17.   How is "centration" related to the concept of "conservation?"

18.   Explain the major criticisms of Piaget's theory.

19.   How does the information-processing approach to cognitive development differ from Piaget's approach?

20.   Describe the following five important factors that information-processing theorists believe influence children's cognitive efficiency:

Processing speed

Automatic processing

Knowledge base

Cognitive strategies

Metacognition

21.   How does Case's model integrate Piagetian and information-processing views of cognitive development?

22.   What is "psychomotor slowing?" How can this affect cognitive performance in the elderly?

23.   How does memory change in the elderly? What aspects of memory decline with age? What aspects are relatively unaffected by age?

24.   In what ways do fluid intelligence and crystallized intelligence change with increasing age?

25.   What are the characteristics and possible causes of Alzheimer's disease?

26.   What evidence is there to support the notion of a critical period for language acquisition?

27.   Describe the progression of children's speech from babbling to grammatical speech.

PART TWO: REVIEW AND LEARN
Key Terms, Fill-In Exercises, Application and Using What You Have Learned

Before doing the exercises below, review the information you learned in this chapter. Reread the work you did in part one of this study guide chapter, plus the interim summaries and end-of-chapter summary in your textbook. Review any problem areas. Once you feel comfortable with the material, do the following exercises without referring to your notes or textbook. If you have difficulty with a term or question, mark it and come back to it. When you have finished an exercise, go back to your notes and the textbook to find the answers to the questions that gave you difficulty. Finally, check your answers (key terms against the textbook and the rest against the answer key).

KEY TERMS

Upon completion of Chapter 13, you should be able to define the following terms.

Developmental psychology   _____

_____

Maturation   _____

_____

Critical periods   _____

_____

Sensitive periods   _____

_____

Stages   _____

_____

Cross-sectional studies _____

_____

Cohort effects _____

_____

Longitudinal studies _____

_____

Sequential studies _____

_____

Teratogens _____

_____

Puberty _____

_____

Presbycusis _____

_____

Ageism _____

_____

Intermodal processing _____

_____

Infantile amnesia _____

_____

Assimilation _____

_____

Schema _____

_____

Accommodation _____

_____

Equilibration _____

_____

Structure of thought _____

_____

Sensorimotor stage _____

_____

Object permanence _____

_____

Egocentric _____

_____

Preoperational stage _____

_____

Operations _____

_____

Concrete operational stage _____

_____

Conservation _____

_____

Formal operational stage   _____

_____

Automatization   _____

_____

Knowledge base   _____

_____

Metacognition   _____

_____

Neo-Piagetian theorists   _____

_____

Psychomotor slowing   _____

_____

Dementia   _____

_____

Alzheimer's disease   _____

_____

Babbling   _____

_____

Telegraphic speech   _____

_____

FILL-IN EXERCISES

Fill in the word or words that best fit in the spaces below.

1. Studies of children who have experienced extreme deprivation during their early years provide evidence for _____ periods in humans, times that are important to subsequent development, although perhaps not absolutely critical for future psychological growth.

2. Some psychologists view development as occurring in stages, where behavior at one stage is not just quantitatively different from behavior at another stage, but _____ different.

3. Cross-sectional studies are most useful when _____ effects (i.e., differences among age groups associated with differences in culture) are minimal.

4. A _____ design combines cross-sectional and _____ comparisons, solving most of the problems of both of these types of design.

5. The first two weeks after conception are referred to as the _____ period.

6. The _____ period begins at about the ninth week of prenatal development.

7. _____ are environmental agents that can harm a developing fetus or embryo.

8. When touched on its cheek, an infant turns its head and opens its mouth to suck. This pattern of behavior is referred to as the _____ _____.

9. In general, the development of motor skills in infants progress from _____ to _____.

10. *Early* onset of puberty tends to be associated with _____ *(more/less)* distress for boys than for girls.

11. For women the most dramatic physical change of middle adulthood is _____.

12. Many older people experience _____ -- the inability to hear high-frequency sounds.

13. The visual acuity of the newborn is estimated to be approximately _____, but improves to approximately _____ by six months.

14. Research over the last 25 years suggests that infants are far more capable of _____ _____ -- the ability to associate sensations of an object from different senses or to match their own actions to behaviors they have observed visually – than anyone would have expected.

15. Most people completely lack explicit memory for events before age 3 or 4, a phenomenon known as _____ _____.

16.   Interpreting actions or events in terms of one's present schemas is referred to as _____, whereas _____ refers to the modification of schemas to fit reality.

17.   Piaget's _____ stage lasts from birth until about 2 years of age.

18.   The preoperational stage is characterized by the emergence of _____ thought.

19.   _____ refers to the preoperational child's tendency to focus on one perceptually striking feature of an object without considering other features that might be relevant.

20.   According to Piaget, once children reach the third stage of development, they are able to understand the concept of _____ -- that basic properties of an object or situation remain stable even though superficial properties may be changed.

21.   In the _____ operational stage children are capable of mentally manipulating abstract as well as concrete objects, events, and ideas.

22.   In contrast to Piaget's theory which focuses on changes occurring in stages, the information-processing perspective focuses on changes that are _____.

23.   Compared to adults, children's _____ _____ (their accumulated knowledge) are limited because of their relative inexperience with life.

24.   _____ refers to the process of thinking about thinking.

25.   Theorists who attempt to integrate Piaget's theory with information-processing views are sometimes referred to as _____-Piagetian theorists.

26.   One of the clearest changes that accompanies aging is _____ _____, an increase in the time required for processing and acting on information.

27.   _____ _____ is a progressive and incurable illness, that occurs later in life, and causes severe impairment of memory, reasoning, language, and behavior.

28.   In acquiring language, one of the first things infants must learn is to _____ the continuous streams of speech they hear into units, so they can distinguish one phoneme, morpheme, word, or phrase from another.

29.   Babies' first recognizable speech sounds are called _____.

30.   Young children characteristically use _____ _____ -- utterances composed of only the most essential words for meaning.

APPLICATION

Situation

Mickey and his older brother Dave are having lunch. When their mother gives them their juice, Mickey's glass is short and fat, while Dave's is tall and thin. Although their mother is careful to pour the same amount of juice into each glass, Mickey complains that Dave got more. Their mother gets a short, fat glass from the cupboard and, while Mickey watches, pours Dave's juice from the tall, thin glass into the new short, fat one. Mickey says "That's better, now they're the same." After watching his mother pour the juice from one glass into the other, Dave just sits there chuckling. He whispers to his mother, "Boy, did you ever fool Mickey! It's the same amount of juice in both glasses!"

Questions to answer

1. Which of Piaget's stages of cognitive development most likely describes Mickey? How about Dave?

2. What does Dave realize that Mickey doesn't? What is this concept called?

3. According to Piaget's theory, what is it that causes Mickey to think there is more juice in the second glass? What is this process called?

USING WHAT YOU HAVE LEARNED

The chapter discusses the phenomenon of *ageism*, a prejudice against old people. It describes how subjects in a priming experiment more readily associated negative traits with the word "old" and positive traits with the word "young." These findings could reflect the stereotypes people apply to the elderly. Stereotypical beliefs about old people are actually relatively common. To get an idea of these beliefs, ask several of your friends what "old" people are like and how they differ from young people.

1. What seem to be the most common stereotypical beliefs?

2. Is there an age difference in beliefs? Do older people have the same beliefs as younger people? If they do, could these actually be a self-fulfilling prophecy?

3. Are any of these beliefs based on fact? Compare people's beliefs with what you have read about aging in this chapter. How accurate are people's beliefs?

4. Does providing objective information about aging alter people's beliefs. A good way to answer this would be to consider your own beliefs *before* and *after* reading Chapter 13. Did they change?

PART THREE: TEST AND KNOW
SAMPLE TEST QUESTIONS

Test how well you have learned this chapter's material by answering the sample test questions. You may wish to mark your answers on a separate sheet of paper so you can reuse this test for exam review. Once you have completed the exam, check your answers and then go back to your notes and the textbook to review questions you found difficult.

1.   When considering the roles of nature and nurture, the question(s) asked by developmental psychologists is (are)

      a.   *Which* is more important in development-- nature or nurture?
      b.   *How much* does each contribute to development?
      c.   *How* do nature and nurture contribute interactively to development?
      d.   all of the above

2.   Relatively discrete steps in development, through which everyone passes in the same sequence, are referred to as

      a.   sensitive periods
      b.   critical periods
      c.   cohorts
      d.   stages

3.   A research design used by developmental psychologists, which follows multiple cohorts longitudinally, is referred to as a

      a.   sequential study
      b.   cross-sectional study
      c.   longitudinal study
      d.   cohort study

4.   By about _____ weeks, the fetus is capable of sustaining life on its own.

      a.   16   b.   22
      c.   28   d.   32

5.   Physical deformities, as well as learning disabilities, behavior problems, and attention difficulties are associated with prenatal exposure to

      a.   alcohol
      b.   iron
      c.   crack cocaine
      d.   nicotine

6.   Which of the following does *NOT* decrease in older adults?

      a.   ability to hear high-frequencies
      b.   crystallized intelligence
      c.   sexual desire
      d.   visual sensitivity to contrasts

7.   Which of the following responses have been used to assess infant perception?

      a.   rooting reflex and sucking
      b.   orienting reflex and fixation time
      c.   equilibration and disequilibration
      d.   assimilation and accommodation

8.   Piaget referred to the process of modifying schemas to fit reality as

      a.   adaptation
      b.   accommodation
      c.   assimilation
      d.   equilibration

9.   For Piaget, the driving force behind cognitive development is

      a.   assimilation
      b.   accommodation
      c.   equilibration
      d.   schemas

10.   A major achievement of the sensorimotor stage is the development of

      a.   decentration
      b.   conservation
      c.   operations
      d.   object permanence

11.   Little Stacey loves playing peek-a-boo. Her favorite part is to cover her eyes with her hands and then call out "Nobody can't see me!". Stacey is likely in which of Piaget's stages of cognitive development?

      a.   formal operational
      b.   preoperational
      c.   sensorimotor
      d.   concrete operational

12.   "If Louise is older than Carol, and Carol is older than Christine, which girl is the youngest?" This type of question requires an understanding of

a.   centration
b.   conservation
c.   egocentrism
d.   transitivity

13.   During which stage are children first able to readily solve problems like the one above?

a.   formal operational
b.   sensorimotor
c.   preoperational
d.   concrete operational

14.   Children's understanding of the way they perform cognitive tasks, such as remembering, learning, and solving problems, is referred to as

a.   metacognition
b.   cognitive strategies
c.   knowledge base
d.   automatic processing

15.   According to Case, the most important factor in qualitative changes in cognitive development (that is, movement across stages) is an increasing

a.   capacity for abstract thinking
b.   ability to make use of metamemory
c.   capacity for working memory
d.   ability to perform operations

16.   The problems older people have with long-term memory appear largely to be in the

a.   encoding of implicit memories
b.   retrieval of explicit memories
c.   storage of information
d.   area of recognition memory

17.   One of the clearest changes that accompanies aging is

a.   a decline in crystallized intelligence
b.   a decline in abstract reasoning abilities
c.   an erosion of the knowledge base
d.   psychomotor slowing

18.   Fluid intelligence

    a.   peaks in young adulthood, then levels off, and begins declining by mid adulthood
    b.   increases throughout most of life, showing declines only in very old age
    c.   begins declining shortly after the preschool period, although the decline is imperceptibly slow at first
    d.   peaks at puberty, then begins a decline that accelerates with age

19.   Alzheimer's patients have abnormally low levels of _____, a neurotransmitter that plays a central role in memory functioning.

    a.   acetylcholine
    b.   serotonin
    c.   norepinephrine
    d.   GABA

20.   Twenty-month-old Danny points to the fridge and says, "Baby want milk." This is an example of

    a.   babbling
    b.   motherese
    c.   telegraphic speech
    d.   bantering

ANSWERS

FILL-IN EXERCISES

1. sensitive   2. qualitatively   3. cohort   4. sequential; longitudinal   5. germinal   6. fetal   7. teratogens
8. rooting reflex   9. head, toe   10. less   11. menopause   12. presbycusis   13. 20/500; 20/100
14. intermodal processing   15. infantile amnesia   16. assimilation; accommodation   17. sensorimotor
18. symbolic   19. centration   20. conservation   21. formal   22. continuous (or quantitative)
23. knowledge bases   24. metacognition   25. neo   26. psychomotor slowing   27. Alzheimer's disease
28. segment   29. babbling   30. telegraphic speech

APPLICATION

1. Mickey is preoperational. Dave is concrete or formal operational.

2. Dave realizes that the amount of juice in the glass has remained the same, even though the size and shape of the glass have changed. In other words, the basic properties of an object remain stable even though its superficial properties may be changed. This is referred to as *conservation*

3. Mickey focuses only on one aspect of the glass -- its height, and ignores the difference between the two glasses in width. *Centration*

SAMPLE TEST QUESTIONS

1.	c	11.	b
2.	d	12.	d
3.	a	13.	d
4.	c	14.	a
5.	a	15.	c
6.	b	16.	b
7.	b	17.	d
8.	b	18.	a
9.	c	19.	a
10.	d	20.	c

Chapter 14
Social Development

PART ONE: PRE-READ AND WORK
Outline and Learning Objectives

Pre-read this chapter's table of contents and end-of-chapter summary. Then, use the outline segment-by-segment to help you work through the chapter. Jot down your own questions, comments, and notes in the space provided. Make a note of key terms and of difficult areas that you will need to review (include page numbers). Then, answer the questions in the learning objectives section that follows. Check off those you are confident that you can answer well. Re-read the material in the text for the questions about which you are less confident. Record the important points from your reading in the space below each question.

OUTLINE

Attachment

Attachment in Infancy

Individual Differences in Attachment Patterns

From Brain to Behavior: Temperament, Experience, and Their Interaction in the Development of Attachment Styles

Implications of Attachment for Later Development

Socialization

The Role of Parents

The Role of Culture

A Global Vista: Parental Acceptance and Rejection in Cross-Cultural Perspective

Socialization of Gender

Peer Relationships

Friendships

Sibling Relationships

Development of Social Cognition

The Evolving Self-Concept

Concepts of Others

Perspective-Taking and Theory of Mind

Children's Understanding of Gender

Moral Development

The Role of Cognition

The Role of Emotion

Commentary: Making Sense of Moral Development

Social Development Across the Lifespan

Erikson's Theory of Psychosocial Development

Development from Adolescence through Old Age

LEARNING OBJECTIVES

Upon completion of Chapter 14, you should be able to answer the following questions.

1. What is imprinting? How is it similar to attachment?

2. How do the Strange Situation behaviors of infants with secure, avoidant, ambivalent, and disorganized attachment styles differ?

3. What are internal working models of relationships?

4. How may temperament and experience influence attachment?

5. How does the later adjustment of securely attached infants differ from that of insecurely attached infants?

6. What is meant by adult attachment style? How is the attachment style of parents related to that of their infants?

7. Can individuals overcome the effects of early negative attachment experiences?

8. What are the characteristics and effects of each of the three styles of parenting identified by Diana Baumrind?

9. Discuss how parental acceptance and rejection may differ across cultures yet be similar in their effects.

10.   What role do adults play in the socialization of gender roles?

11.   What changes take place across age in the meaning of friendship to children and in the roles that friends play?

12.   How do rejected children differ from neglected children?

13.   What are the characteristics of sibling relationships?

14.   How do children's descriptions of themselves and others change across age?.

15.   How is the development of theory of mind related to perspective taking?

16.   What changes occur across age in children's perspective taking?

17.   Compare between the following three stages of children's understanding of gender: gender identity, gender stability, gender constancy.

18.   What are gender schemas?

19.   Discuss the biological/evolutionary and cultural/social-learning explanations for gender differences in aggression and nurturance.

20.   How do Piaget's stages of morality of constraint and morality of cooperation differ?

21.   What are Kohlberg's three levels of moral reasoning? Provide examples of answers to the Heinz dilemma for each level.

22.   According to the social-cognitive view, how is prosocial behavior acquired?

23.   Outline the sequence of judgments that comprise the information-processing model of moral decision making.

24.   Explain the psychodynamic view of moral development.

25.   How does empathy develop in children?

26.   What are the advantages and shortcomings associated with the cognitive and emotional approaches to moral development?

27.   What is the major crisis or developmental task of each of Erikson's eight stages of psychosocial development?

28.   How do the conflict and continuity models differ in their view of adolescence?

29.   What factors have been found to have the potential to interfere with marital intimacy and satisfaction with marriage?

30.   Is there really a "midlife crisis?"

31.   What factors have been found to predict happiness and satisfaction in old age?

PART TWO: REVIEW AND LEARN
Key Terms, Fill-In Exercises, Application and Using What You Have Learned

Before doing the exercises below, review the information you learned in this chapter. Reread the work you did in part one of this study guide chapter, plus the interim summaries and end-of-chapter summary in your textbook. Review any problem areas. Once you feel comfortable with the material, do the following exercises without referring to your notes or textbook. If you have difficulty with a term or question, mark it and come back to it. When you have finished an exercise, go back to your notes and the textbook to find the answers to the questions that gave you difficulty. Finally, check your answers (key terms against the textbook and the rest against the answer key).

KEY TERMS

Social development   _____

_____

Attachment   _____

_____

Imprinting   _____

_____

Separation anxiety   _____

_____

Secure attachment style   _____

_____

Avoidant attachment style   _____

_____

Ambivalent attachment style   _____

_____

Disorganized attachment style   _____

_____

Internal working models   _____

_____

Adult attachment   _____

_____

Socialization   _____

_____

Authoritarian parents   _____

_____

Permissive parents   _____

_____

Authoritative parents   _____

_____

Uninvolved parents   _____

_____

Gender roles   _____

_____

Gender _____

_____

Sex typing _____

_____

Rejected children _____

_____

Neglected children _____

_____

Social cognition _____

_____

Self-concept _____

_____

Perspective-taking _____

_____

Theory of mind _____

_____

Gender identity _____

_____

Gender stability _____

_____

Gender constancy _____

_____

Gender schemas _____

_____

Sex-role ideology   _____

_____

Morality of constraint   _____

_____

Morality of cooperation   _____

_____

Preconventional morality_____

_____

Conventional morality   _____

_____

Postconventional morality   _____

_____

Prosocial behavior   _____

_____

Empathy   _____

_____

Empathic distress   _____

_____

Psychosocial stages   _____

_____

Developmental task   _____

_____

Basic trust versus mistrust   _____

_____

Autonomy versus shame and doubt   _____

_____

Initiative versus guilt   _____

_____

Industry versus inferiority   _____

_____

Identity versus identity confusion _____

_____

Identity _____

_____

Identity confusion   _____

_____

Initiation rites   _____

_____

Negative identity   _____

_____

Intimacy versus isolation   _____

_____

Generativity versus stagnation   _____

_____

Generativity   _____

_____

Stagnation   _____

_____

Integrity versus despair   _____

_____

Conflict model   _____

_____

Continuity model   _____

_____

FILL-IN EXERCISES

Fill in the word or words that best fit in the spaces below.

1.   The term _____ refers to the tendency of young animals of certain species to follow an animal to which they were exposed during a sensitive period early in their lives.

2.   The attachment figure serves as a safe _____ from which children can explore the environment, and to whom they can periodically return for "emotional refueling."

3.   Babies visually recognize their mother at about _____ months of age and, by about _____ or _____ months recognize and greet their mothers and other attachment figures from across the room.

4.   Cross-cultural research, as well as research with blind infants, suggest a _____ basis for separation anxiety.

5.   In the Strange Situation, infants who welcome their mother after her absence and seek closeness with her have a _____ attachment style.

6.   Bowlby proposed that infants develop _____ _____ models, or mental representations of attachment relationships, which form the basis for expectations in close relationships.

7. Adults with an attachment style characterized as _____ (similar to the disorganized style seen in infancy) have difficulty speaking coherently about attachment figures from their past and have generally been unable to cope with losses or other traumatic experiences from their past.

8. _____ involves learning the rules, beliefs, values, skills, attitudes, and behavior patterns of society.

9. Parents who place a high value on obedience and respect for authority are described as _____ parents; those who impose virtually no controls on their children are referred to as _____ parents; while those who set and enforce standards, but also encourage give and take are called _____ parents. Finally, _____ parents consistently place their own needs above the needs of their child.

10. While the term sex refers to a biological classification based on genetic and anatomical differences, the term _____ refers to the psychological meaning of being male or female, which is influenced by _____.

11. Friendships marked by commitment and reciprocity (sharing and give and take) first begin to emerge around age _____.

12. Adolescents are more concerned than younger children with _____ in friendships.

13. Children who are rarely picked by their classmates as either someone they really like or someone they really dislike are referred to as _____ children.

14. Children's understanding of themselves, others, and relationships is referred to as _____ _____.

15. The term _____ _____ refers to an organized view of ourselves or way of representing information about the self.

16. _____ _____ refers to the ability to understand other people's viewpoints.

17. The ability to categorize oneself as either male or female is called _____ _____ and usually is attained by about _____ years of age.

18. Gender _____ occurs when children learn that a person's gender cannot be altered by changes in appearance or activities.

19. Gender _____ are mental representations that associate psychological characteristics with each sex.

20. _____-_____ _____ refers to beliefs about the appropriate behavior of the sexes.

21.   The term _____ refers to the set of rules people use to balance the conflicting interests of themselves and others.

22.   Viewing social rules as unchanging and unchangeable is one of the characteristics of the stage Piaget called the morality of _____.

23.   According to Kohlberg's theory, the desire to gain the approval or avoid the disapproval of others is one characteristic of the level of _____ morality.

24.   According to the _____ model, moral reasoning involves making a series of sequential judgments about whether an act is immoral and whether it deserves punishment.

25.   The psychodynamic view of moral development proposes that children start out relatively _____, or self-centered and interested in gratifying their own needs.

26.   Discrepancies between what people feel they should do and what they contemplate or observe themselves doing result in _____.

27.   As children become better able to distinguish their own thoughts and feelings from those of others, they begin to experience genuine _____ distress – feeling upset for another person – which motivates moral or prosocial behavior.

28.   Erikson's model is comprised of eight _____ stages of development.

29.   The third of Erikson's stages is called "*initiative versus* _____." The next stage is "_____ *versus inferiority.*"

30.   Some adolescents adopt a _____ _____, taking on a role that society defines as bad, but which provides them with a sense that at least they are something.

31.   To Erikson, the opposite of "*generativity*" is _____.

32.   Erikson's final stage is "_____ *versus* _____."

APPLICATION

In Chapter 14, you learned about the challenges or developmental tasks faced by individuals at different stages in their lives, according to Erikson's theory. Each of the descriptions that follow translates one of Erikson's developmental tasks into a conflict faced by a particular individual. For each description, match the psychosocial stage that corresponds to the challenge they're facing. (Note: Some stages appear more than once.)

Psychosocial Stages

Basic Trust versus Mistrust
Autonomy versus Shame and Doubt
Initiative versus Guilt
Industry versus Inferiority

Identity versus Identity Confusion
Intimacy versus Isolation
Generativity versus Stagnation
Integrity versus Despair

Conflicts

1.   Paul is a "professional student." He has studied engineering, general arts, history, psychology, and criminology. Now, he feels maybe he should leave university and try business for a while.

2.   Monica spends a lot of time playing make-believe. She enjoys dressing up in adult clothes, pretending to be the role she dresses as. She loves dreaming up ideas and carrying them out.

3.   Ronny loves sports at school. He's quite athletic and is always trying to show that he's better than anyone else on the soccer team.

4.   Since her kids left home, Diane has been toying with the idea of becoming a scout leader. She thought she'd like all the time she'd have to herself when the kids grew up, but, in fact, she finds her life feels really empty with them gone.

5.   Sarah hangs out with a group of punks. They hang around the shopping plaza doing nothing and seem to delight in offending some of the shoppers by their foul language and appearance.

6.   Ian has been avoiding Jennifer. He likes her and she likes him. But, he's afraid to get too close. Their relationship is starting to get serious and that scares Ian.

7.   Geoff has been having problems with reading at school. Compared to other kids he's far behind. It's especially hard when they take turns reading aloud. He slouches down in his desk and tries to hide so that the teacher won't call on him.

8.   Guy has run a successful TV repair business for 20 years. Last year he sold the business to spend his time teaching TV repair to physically disabled teenagers.

9.   Sonia is always trying to do things on her own. She seems proud of the fact that she can now stand on her own two feet. In fact, she often insists on doing things like feeding herself, even if it means getting the food all over herself.

USING WHAT YOU HAVE LEARNED

A group of students has just covered social development in their Introduction to Psychology course. The topic of attachment in infancy was particularly interesting, and a topic they hadn't given much thought to, previously. The students get into a discussion concerning whether attachment is important and what role a mother plays in her infant's attachment. Your job is to decide whether each student's opinion is accurate or not, based on your readings in the text.

- **Student #1:** "As far as I'm concerned, attachment isn't very important. Sure you can't just ignore babies; you have to feed them and change them. But all this 'lovey-dovey' stuff just makes their parents feel good. It's not important for the baby. How babies feel about their mothers isn't important in the long run."

- **Student #2:** "Well, I think attachment is VERY important! Once a baby has formed an insecure attachment, there isn't very much you can do to change things. They'll be messed up for life!"

- **Student #3:** "I've been thinking about what causes insecure attachment and it's got to be the mother's fault. Mothers are totally to blame if their baby is insecurely attached. It has to do with how they treat their baby, and that's all there is to it."

- **Student #4:** "I think there's too much 'mother-bashing' that goes on when people talk about attachment. Everybody says it's the mother's fault. So if a baby isn't securely attached, who gets blamed? The mother! What a load of guilt to put on someone. What about the baby? Are babies all the same? Aren't some babies more easily scared than others, no matter what their mother does?"

PART THREE: TEST AND KNOW
SAMPLE TEST QUESTIONS

Test how well you have learned this chapter's material by answering the sample test questions. You may wish to mark your answers on a separate sheet of paper so you can reuse this test for exam review. Once you have completed the exam, check your answers and then go back to your notes and the textbook to review questions you found difficult.

1.   Separation anxiety emerges at about the same time as

   a.   the infant is able to stand alone
   b.   the infant begins to walk
   c.   the infant is weaned
   d.   the infant begins to crawl

2. Sally was very upset when her mother left her alone in the Strange Situation. When her mother returned, Sally was angry and rejecting, yet at the same time sought to be close to her. Sally's attachment pattern is best described as

 a. disorganized
 b. securely attached
 c. ambivalent
 d. avoidant

3. The temperamental variable that is most highly predictive of attachment status across several studies is:

 a. slowness to warm up
 b. susceptibility to stress
 c. negative affect
 d. empathic distress

4. Adults who dismiss the importance of attachment relationships or offer idealized generalizations about their parents, but are unable to back them up with specific examples, tend to display a(n) _____ adult attachment style.

 a. secure
 b. ambivalent
 c. unresolved
 d. avoidant

5. Parents who place high value on obedience and respect for authority and do not encourage discussion of *why* particular behaviors are important are described as

 a. authoritarian
 b. permissive
 c. authoritative
 d. disorganized

6. Low self-reliance and poor impulse control is associated with which parenting style?

 a. authoritarian
 b. permissive
 c. authoritative
 d. disorganized

7. Parents often treat their sons and daughters differently from an early age. Girls in Europe and North America, in contrast to boys, receive more

 a. punishment.
 b. encouragement to compete.
 c. pressure not to cry.
 d. warmth, affection, and trust.

8. Neglected children tend to be

 a. ignored by their peers
 b. disliked by their peers
 c. hostile and aggressive
 d. at risk for later delinquency

9.   When asked to describe himself, Sid replies "I'm good at math, and I'm the best skateboarder in my school." Based on his description, Sid is likely around

a.   3 years of age   b.   6 years of age
c.   9 years of age   d.   17 years of age

10.   In the game "Decoy and Defender" a child simply moves her flag carrier as quickly as possible across the board, totally failing to take into account her opponent's perspective. Such an egocentric strategy would be typical of a(n)

a.   1- to 2-year-old child
b.   3- to 6-year-old child
c.   6- to 8-year-old child
d.   8- to 10-year-old child

11.   Gender constancy refers to children's

a.   tendency to play and form friendships primarily with same-sex peers
b.   realization that their gender remains constant over time
c.   ability to categorize themselves and others according to gender
d.   realization that a person's gender cannot be altered by changes in appearance or activities

12.   Mental representations that associate psychological characteristics with each sex are referred to as

a.   gender roles
b.   gender schemas
c.   sex typing
d.   gender constancy

13.   The majority of preindustrial societies socialize boys from an early age to be

a.   self-reliant   b.   self-restrained
c.   responsible   d.   obedient

14.   When one child tries to change the rules to a game of marbles, the child she is playing with gets very upset, shouting "You're not allowed to break the rules!" The second child is likely at which of Piaget's stages of moral development?

a.   morality of cooperation
b.   postconventional morality
c.   morality of constraint
d.   conventional morality

15.   After listening to the dilemma of Heinz and the druggist, an individual responds that Heinz should steal the drug, because the value of human life is far more important than obeying the law. This answer is characteristic of which of Kohlberg's levels of moral development?

   a.   morality of cooperation   b.   postconventional morality
   c.   morality of constraint   d.   conventional morality

16.   According to cognitive-social theories of moral development, children learn that certain acts are wrong and will be punished because they

   a.   are punished for the act
   b.   see someone else punished
   c.   are told they will be punished
   d.   all of the above

17.   When 13-month-old Fred saw his mother crying, he offered her his soother as a way of trying to comfort her. Fred's behavior was likely motivated by the feeling of

   a.   empathic distress   b.   guilt
   c.   narcissism   d.   vicarious punishment

18.   Kohlberg's theory of moral development has been criticized as biased against women because

   a.   Kohlberg never examined the moral reasoning of women in his research
   b.   women's moral concerns are more likely to center on issues of care and responsibility, rather than justice
   c.   women's moral concerns are more likely to center on issues of justice rather than care and responsibility
   d.   men are very concerned with obeying the rules, whereas women are not

19.   In Erikson's theory, children who have difficulty with this stage may be highly self-critical or may become rigid and constricted as a way of dealing with impulses they have come to view as bad.

   a.   initiative vs. guilt
   b.   trust vs. mistrust
   c.   industry vs. inferiority
   d.   autonomy vs. shame and doubt

20.   According to Erikson, _____ occurs when an individual fails to develop a coherent and enduring sense of self, and has difficulty committing to roles, values, people, and occupational choices.

   a.   the midlife crisis
   b.   despair
   c.   identity confusion
   d.   stagnation

ANSWERS

FILL-IN EXERCISES

1. imprinting 2. base 3. three; five, six 4. maturational 5. secure 6. internal working 7. unresolved
8. socialization 9. authoritarian; permissive; authoritative; uninvolved 10. gender; learning 11. three
12. intimacy 13. neglected 14. social cognition 15. self-concept 16. perspective taking 17. gender
identity; two 18. constancy 19. schemas 20. sex-role ideology 21. morality 22. constraint
23. conventional 24. information-processing 25. narcissistic 26. guilt 27. empathic 28. psychosocial
29. guilt; industry 30. negative identity 31. stagnation 32. integrity; despair

APPLICATION

1. identity versus identity diffusion 2. initiative versus guilt 3. industry versus inferiority 4. generativity
versus stagnation 5. identity versus identity diffusion 6. intimacy versus isolation 7. industry versus
inferiority 8. generativity versus stagnation 9. autonomy versus shame and doubt

USING WHAT YOU HAVE LEARNED

1. No -   Attachment *is* important. It is related to later social and academic competence, and may be influential throughout life, perhaps influencing adult attachment.
2. No -   While disturbed attachment does predict later adjustment problems, this is not always the case, nor is attachment style unchangeable.
3. No -   While maternal responsiveness is very important, it is not the only variable to affect attachment. Temperament and environmental factors also are important.
4. Yes-   Temperament may be very important. The three infant temperaments – easy, difficult, and slow-to-warm-up – may correspond to secure, ambivalent, and avoidant attachment styles. Inborn timidity or fearfulness may also be related.

SAMPLE TEST QUESTIONS

1.	d	11.	d
2.	c	12.	b
3.	c	13.	a
4.	d	14.	c
5.	a	15.	b
6.	b	16.	d
7.	d	17.	a
8.	a	18.	b
9.	c	19.	a
10.	b	20.	c

Chapter 15
Psychological Disorders

PART ONE: PRE-READ AND WORK
Outline and Learning Objectives

Pre-read this chapter's table of contents and end-of-chapter summary. Then, use the outline segment-by-segment to help you work through the chapter. Jot down your own questions, comments, and notes in the space provided. Make a note of key terms and of difficult areas that you will need to review (include page numbers). Then, answer the questions in the learning objectives section that follows. Check off those you are confident that you can answer well. Re-read the material in the text for the questions about which you are less confident. Record the important points from your reading in the space below each question.

OUTLINE

The Cultural Context of Psychopathology

Culture and Psychopathology

Is Mental Illness Nothing but a Cultural Construction?

Contemporary Approaches to Psychopathology

Psychodynamic Perspective

Cognitive-Behavioral Perspective

Biological Approach

Systems Approach

Evolutionary Perspective

Descriptive Diagnoses: DSM-IV and Psychopathological Syndromes

DSM-IV

Disorders Usually First Diagnosed in Infancy, Childhood, or Adolescence

Substance-Related Disorders

Schizophrenia

From Brain to Behavior: The Biology of Schizophrenia

Mood Disorders

A Global Vista: Depression on a Hopi Reservation

Anxiety Disorders

Eating Disorders

Dissociative Disorders

Personality Disorders

One Step Further: Are Mental Disorders Really Distinct?

LEARNING OBJECTIVES

Upon completion of Chapter 15, you should be able to answer the following questions.

1.   How is psychopathology influenced by culture?

2.   What is labeling theory? How did the research Rosenhan conducted in mental institutions support this view of psychopathology?

3.   What criticisms have been voiced concerning labeling theory approaches?

4.   What are the differences between neuroses, personality disorders, and psychoses?

5.   What are the three questions that comprise a psychodynamic formulation?

6.   How do the behavioral and cognitive approaches conceptualize psychopathology?

7.   How does the biological approach conceptualize mental disorders?

8.   How do psychologists with a systems approach view psychopathology?

9.   How would psychopathology be explained by evolutionary psychologists?

10.   What are the five axes that make up DSM-IV's multiaxial system of diagnosis?

11.   What are the major characteristics of attention-deficit hyperactivity disorder (ADHD) and of conduct disorder?

12.   How do both genetic and environmental factors account for the findings that alcoholism runs in families?

13.   What has recent research shown concerning adolescents who use marijuana?

14.   What are the major characteristics of schizophrenia?

15.   Describe the positive and negative symptoms of schizophrenia.

16.   What is the dopamine hypothesis? How does it account for both the positive and negative symptoms of schizophrenia?

17.   Discuss the evidence indicating that both biological and environmental factors contribute to schizophrenia.

18.   What are the differences between major depressive disorder, dysthymic disorder, and bipolar disorder?

19.   Discuss the contributions of genetic factors, neurotransmitters, and environmental factors to depression.

20.   What are four types of cognitive distortions or errors that Beck describes as typical of depressed thinking? Provide examples for each.

21.   How does the psychodynamic view of depression differ from the cognitive view?

22.   How are gender and culture related to the way people view and experience depression?

23.   Describe the symptoms of the following anxiety disorders:

Phobia

Social phobia

Panic disorder

Agoraphobia

Obsessive-compulsive disorder

Posttraumatic stress disorder (PTSD)

24.   How do genetic vulnerability, stress, and personality characteristics contribute to anxiety?

25.   How does David Barlow's model explain the development of panic attacks?

26.   What are the characteristics of anorexia nervosa and bulimia? What are the roles of biological, environmental, and personality factors in the development of these disorders?

27.   What are the central features of dissociative disorders?

28.   Provide a very brief description of each of the following personality disorders:

Paranoid

Schizoid

Schizotypal

Antisocial

Borderline

Histrionic

Narcissistic

Avoidant

Dependent

Obsessive-compulsive

29   What are the symptoms of borderline personality disorder and antisocial personality disorder? What similarities and differences are there in the etiology of each disorder?

30   Why is it difficult to distinguish the roles of nature and nurture in the etiology of psychological disturbances?

PART TWO: REVIEW AND LEARN
Key Terms, Fill-In Exercises, Application and Using What You Have Learned

Before doing the exercises below, review the information you learned in this chapter. Reread the work you did in part one of this study guide chapter, plus the interim summaries and end-of-chapter summary in your textbook. Review any problem areas. Once you feel comfortable with the material, do the following exercises without referring to your notes or textbook. If you have difficulty with a term or question, mark it and come back to it. When you have finished an exercise, go back to your notes and the textbook to find the answers to the questions that gave you difficulty. Finally, check your answers (key terms against the textbook and the rest against the answer key).

KEY TERMS

Psychopathology _____

_____

Labeling theory _____

_____

Neuroses _____

_____

Personality disorders _____

_____

Psychoses _____

_____

Etiology_____

_____

Psychodynamic formulation _____

_____

Cognitive-behavioral _____

_____

Diathesis-stress model _____

_____

Systems approach _____

_____

System _____

_____

Family systems model _____

_____

Family homeostatic mechanisms_____

_____

Family roles _____

_____

Family boundaries _____

_____

Family alliances _____

_____

Descriptive diagnosis _____

_____

Clinical syndromes _____

_____

DSM-IV _____

_____

Multiaxial system of diagnosis _____

_____

Attention-deficit hyperactivity disorder (ADHD) _____

_____

Conduct disorder _____

_____

Substance-related disorders _____

_____

Alcoholism _____

_____

Schizophrenia _____

_____

Delusions _____

_____

Hallucinations _____

_____

Loosening of associations _____

_____

Positive symptoms _____

_____

Negative symptoms _____

_____

Dopamine hypothesis _____

_____

Ventricles _____

_____

Expressed emotion _____

_____

Mood disorders _____

_____

Major depressive disorder _____

_____

Dysthymic disorder _____

_____

Bipolar disorder _____

_____

Manic episodes _____

_____

Unipolar depression _____

_____

Negative triad _____

_____

Cognitive Distortions   _____

_____

Anxiety disorders   _____

_____

Generalized anxiety disorder   _____

_____

Phobia _____

_____

Social phobia   _____

_____

Panic disorder   _____

_____

Agoraphobia   _____

_____

Obsessive-compulsive disorder   _____

_____

Obsessions   _____

_____

Compulsions   _____

_____

Posttraumatic stress disorder (PTSD)   _____

_____

Anorexia nervosa _____

_____

Bulimia _____

_____

Dissociation _____

_____

Dissociative disorders _____

_____

Dissociative identity disorder _____

_____

Personality disorder _____

_____

Borderline personality disorder _____

_____

Antisocial personality disorder _____

_____

FILL-IN EXERCISES

Fill in the word or words that best fit in the spaces below.

1.   Thomas Szasz argued that mental illness is a _____.

2.   According to _____ theory, diagnosis is a way of stigmatizing individuals a society considers deviant.

3.   Psychodynamic psychologists use information they gather about the patient to make a _____ _____ -- a set of hypotheses about the patient's personality structure and the meaning of the symptom.

4.   In clinical psychology, many practitioners consider themselves _____-_____, integrating an understanding of classical and operant conditioning with a cognitive-social perspective.

5.   From a cognitive perspective, psychopathology reflects dysfunctional _____ that maintain dysfunctional behaviors and emotions.

6.   The _____-_____ model holds that people with an underlying vulnerability may exhibit symptoms under stressful circumstances.

7.   Systems theorists refer to the methods family members use to preserve equilibrium in a family as family _____ mechanisms.

8.   Family _____ are parts individuals play in repetitive family "dramas" -- according to system theorists.

9.   In descriptive diagnosis, constellations of symptoms that tend to occur together are referred to as clinical _____.

10.   DSM-IV uses a _____ system of diagnosis, which places symptoms in their biological and social context by evaluating patients along five axes.

11.   Attention-deficit hyperactivity disorder is characterized by _____, _____, and _____ inappropriate for the child's age.

12.   Attention-deficit hyperactivity disorder is more prevalent in _____ *(males/females)* than in _____ *(males/females)* .

13.   A relatively common disturbance of childhood is _____ disorder, characterized by persistent violation of societal norms and the rights of others.

14.   As in other Western countries, the third largest health problem in the United States today, following heart disease and cancer, is _____.

15. Individuals with schizophrenia often suffer from _____ -- false beliefs firmly held despite evidence to the contrary.

16. Perceptual experiences that distort or occur without external stimulation, common in schizophrenia, are referred to as _____.

17. _____ symptoms are relatively chronic symptoms of schizophrenia that include flat affect (blunted emotional response), lack of motivation, socially inappropriate behavior and withdrawal from relationships, and intellectual impairments such as impoverished thought.

18. One abnormality observed in the brains of individuals with schizophrenia is brain atrophy or neuronal loss, reflected in enlargement of the fluid-filled cavities of the brain called _____, indicating that the neural regions surrounding them have degenerated.

19. A particularly important environmental in schizophrenia is _____ _____ -- the tendency of family interactions to be characterized by criticism, hostile interchanges, and emotional overinvolvement or intrusiveness by family members.

20. _____ describes a loss of interest in pleasurable activities, characteristic of major depressive disorder.

21. Individuals with _____ disorder often experience both depression and mania.

22. The neurotransmitters _____ and _____ have been implicated in both major depression and bipolar disorders.

23. According to Beck, _____ _____ involve a depressed person's transforming neutral or positive information in a negative direction.

24. Statistics indicate that _____ (*men/women*) are about twice as likely to suffer from depression as _____ (*men/women*).

25. At any given point in time, about _____ percent of the population has at least one irrational fear or _____.

26. _____ is a fear of being in places or situations from which escape might be difficult.

27. _____ are persistent irrational thoughts or ideas that cause distress and interfere with an individual's life.

28. According to David Barlow, as autonomic responses such as quickened pulse, pounding heart, and difficulty breathing become associated with the panic state through classical conditioning, people with panic disorders often develop a fear of _____.

29. Bulimia is characterized by a _____-and-_____ syndrome.

30.   _____ _____ disorder (popularly known as multiple personality disorder) is characterized by at least two separate and distinct personalities existing within the same person.

31.   People with _____ personality disorder have severe trouble in relationships because of a tendency to use people, to be hypersensitive to criticism, to feel entitled to special privileges, and to become rageful when others do not respond to them in ways they find satisfying or appropriate to their status.

USING WHAT YOU HAVE LEARNED

Beck's approach to depression emphasizes cognitive errors in the reasoning of depressed individuals. Below are some hypothetical situations involving such errors. Provide the most appropriate label for each error.

1.   A stranger approaching an individual on the sidewalk suddenly crosses the street and begins walking on the other side. The individual concludes: "He thinks I'm awful and can't stand to walk near me."

2.   After being turned down for one date, a depressed man concludes: "I'm unattractive to women and I'll never get a date."

3.   Ignoring her grade of A- on the midterm exam, a student asked: "Why can't I do *well* in this course?"

4.   After being pulled over for going 10 mph over the limit, a driver concludes: "This is terrible, I'm going to lose my license!" When informed by the police that all he was getting was a warning ticket, he concluded: "It's just as bad, they'll never let me renew my insurance after this!"

5.   After three years of repair-free driving, George's car got a flat tire when he drove over a broken bottle. He said to his friend: "I should never have bought this stupid car. It's nothing but a lemon!"

APPLICATION

Identify the disorder that best describes the following fictitious examples.

1. An 8-year-old boy is having troubles in school. He cannot sit still at his desk, has trouble focusing on class work, and impulsively calls out answers without putting his hand up. He's been getting into arguments and fights lately with other kids, although his teacher thinks it may be due to his negative feelings about school.

2. A writer has periods where she produces so much work that her friends are amazed. She's on an emotional high during her productive periods, and can get by with only a couple of hours of sleep each day. But she has other periods when she can't seem to write anything; she can't concentrate; in fact, she often can't even get out of bed for days at a time. During these times, nothing interests her, even things she usually loves to do.

3. A restaurant worker has a persistent fear that he has inadvertently contaminated the food he is preparing with a poisonous compound. He repeatedly throws out the food and starts from scratch, meticulously writing down every ingredient he adds to the meal.

4. An individual is afraid to leave her house and travel to work because of a fear of experiencing a panic attack on the subway or at the office.

5. A 25-year-old gets into trouble with the law repeatedly for stealing and destroying the property of innocent victims. When caught, he shows no remorse and no concern for the harm he has caused his victims. He is extremely charming, however, and easily finds new victims to con.

6. A college student is extremely anxious about his "performance" in front of others and what others may be thinking of him. The problem is so intense that he often avoids attending classes, in case he might be called upon to answer a question in class.

PART THREE: TEST AND KNOW
SAMPLE TEST QUESTIONS

Test how well you have learned this chapter's material by answering the sample test questions. You may wish to mark your answers on a separate sheet of paper so you can reuse this test for exam review. Once you have completed the exam, check your answers and then go back to your notes and the textbook to review questions you found difficult.

1.   According to psychiatrist Thomas Szasz

   a.   panic disorders represent a fear of fear
   b.   mental illness is a myth
   c.   psychiatric illness is in the eye of the beholder
   d.   the symptoms of any individual are really indicative of disruptions in the individual's family

2.   Psychodynamic theorists distinguish among three broad classes of psychopathology

   a.   neuroses, anxiety disorders, and psychoses
   b.   affective disorders, personality disorders, and psychoses
   c.   dissociative disorders, personality disorders, and psychoses
   d.   neuroses, personality disorders, and psychoses

3.   The descriptive approach embodied in DSM-IV tends to be most compatible with

   a.   a psychodynamic approach to psychopathology
   b.   a disease model of psychopathology
   c.   a cognitive-behavioral approach to psychopathology
   d.   the systems approach to psychopathology

4.   The prevalence of ADHD is estimated at _____ of school-aged children.

   a.   5%
   b.   10%
   c.   15%
   d.   50%

5.   Research suggests that some children with conduct disorder

   a.   are oversensitive to rewards and punishments
   b.   are subject to intense anxiety in social situations
   c.   are relatively unresponsive to conditioning
   d.   frequently display self-mutilating behavior

6.   Perhaps the best predictor of whether someone will develop alcoholism is

     a.   the presence of an anxiety disorder
     b.   a history of conduct disorder or antisocial personality disorder
     c.   the presence of a bipolar disorder
     d.   a family history of alcoholism

7.   The neurotransmitter that seems to be involved in schizophrenia is

     a.   dopamine
     b.   GABA
     c.   norepinephrine
     d.   acetylcholine

8.   One member of a pair of MZ twins is diagnosed with schizophrenia, while the other remains healthy. What are the chances that the offspring of the healthy twin will develop schizophrenia?

     a.   slim, since the parent does not have schizophrenia
     b.   about the same as the chances of anyone else in the general population
     c.   impossible to determine
     d.   about the same as the offspring of the twin with schizophrenia

9.   Too little dopamine in the circuit that projects from the midbrain to the prefrontal cortex is associated with the

     a.   negative symptoms of schizophrenia
     b.   mood fluctuations in seasonal affective disorder
     c.   low conditionability of individuals with antisocial personality disorder
     d.   false alarms associated with anxiety disorders

10.   A chronic, low-level depression lasting more than two years, interrupted by short intervals of normal moods is referred to as

     a.   seasonal affective disorder
     b.   dysthymic disorder
     c.   bipolar depression
     d.   anhedonia

11.   A _____ episode refers to a period of abnormally elevated or expansive mood.

     a.   schizophrenic
     b.   agoraphobic
     c.   manic
     d.   borderline

12.   Beck describes the negative triad as a negative outlook on

    a.   the past, present, and future
    b.   the self, family, and others
    c.   the world, self, and future
    d.   working, loving, and happiness

13.   Unlike cognitive theorists, who focus on faulty cognition, psychodynamic explanations of depression focus on

    a.   distortions
    b.   beliefs
    c.   roles
    d.   motivation

14.   Nightmares, flashbacks, hypervigilance, exaggerated startle responses, and psychological numbness are symptoms associated with

    a.   bipolar disorder
    b.   posttraumatic stress disorder
    c.   obsessive-compulsive disorder
    d.   schizophrenia

15.   Roughly 80% of patients suffering from panic attacks

    a.   describe a negative life event that coincided with their first attack
    b.   report a history of physical or sexual abuse
    c.   attribute negative or malevolent intentions to other people and expect abuse and rejection
    d.   experience extremely unstable interpersonal relationships

16.   What percentage of patients with anorexia are male?

    a.   10%
    b.   25%
    c.   50%
    d.   90%

17.   Disruptions in consciousness, memory, sense of identity, or perception are characteristic of

    a.   panic attacks
    b.   narcissistic personality disorder
    c.   borderline personality disorder
    d.   dissociative disorders

18.   Psychodynamic theorists argue that _____ originates in pathological attachment relationships in early childhood, which lead to attachment problems later in life.

    a.   obsessive-compulsive disorder
    b.   narcissistic personality disorder
    c.   borderline personality disorder
    d.   bulimia

19.   In explaining the development of antisocial personality disorder, both cognitive-behavioral and psychodynamic approaches implicate

    a.   the importance of a sexually abusive male relative
    b.   physical abuse, neglect, and absent or criminal male role models
    c.   the importance of both anxiety and mood disorders in the individual's family
    d.   a high incidence of expressed emotion in the individual's family

20.   Schizoaffective disorder refers to

    a.   a depressive syndrome that occurs primarily in the winter
    b.   a mixture of anxiety and depression
    c.   a disorder that involves attributes of both schizophrenia and psychotic depression
    d.   a disorder characterized by alternating cycles of elation and depression

ANSWERS

FILL-IN EXERCISES

1. myth 2. labeling 3. psychodynamic formulation 4. cognitive-behavioral 5. cognitions 6. diathesis-stress 7. homeostatic 8. roles 9. syndromes 10. multiaxial 11. inattention, impulsivity, hyperactivity 12. males; females 13. conduct 14. alcoholism 15. delusions 16. hallucinations 17. negative 18. ventricles 19. expressed emotion 20. anhedonia 21. bipolar 22. serotonin, norepinephrine 23. cognitive distortions 24. women, men 25. five; phobia 26. agoraphobia 27. obsessions 28. fear 29. binge; purge 30. dissociative identity 31. narcissistic

USING WHAT YOU HAVE LEARNED

1. personalization
2. overgeneralization
3. arbitrary inference
4. magnification
5. arbitrary inference

APPLICATION

1. attention-deficit hyperactivity disorder
2. bipolar disorder
3. obsessive-compulsive disorder
4. agoraphobia
5. antisocial personality disorder
6. social phobia

SAMPLE TEST QUESTIONS

1.	b	11.	c
2.	d	12.	c
3.	b	13.	d
4.	a	14.	b
5.	c	15.	a
6.	d	16.	a
7.	a	17.	d
8.	d	18.	c
9.	a	19.	b
10.	b	20.	c

Chapter 16
Treatment of Psychological Disorders

PART ONE: PRE-READ AND WORK
Outline and Learning Objectives

Pre-read this chapter's table of contents and end-of-chapter summary. Then, use the outline segment-by-segment to help you work through the chapter. Jot down your own questions, comments, and notes in the space provided. Make a note of key terms and of difficult areas that you will need to review (include page numbers). Then, answer the questions in the learning objectives section that follows. Check off those you are confident that you can answer well. Re-read the material in the text for the questions about which you are less confident. Record the important points from your reading in the space below each question.

OUTLINE

Psychodynamic Therapies

Therapeutic Techniques

Varieties of Psychodynamic Therapy

Cognitive-Behavioral Therapies

Basic Principles

Classical Conditioning Techniques

Operant Conditioning Techniques

Modeling and Skills Training

Cognitive Therapy

Humanistic, Group, and Family Therapies

Humanistic Therapies

Group Therapies

Family Therapies

A Global Vista: Culture and Psychotherapy

One Step Further: Psychotherapy Integration

Biological Treatments

From Brain to Behavior: Psychotropic Medications

Antipsychotic Medications

Antidepressant and Mood-Stabilizing Medications

Antianxiety Medications

Electroconvulsive Therapy and Psychosurgery

Evaluating Psychological Treatments

Pharmacotherapy

Psychotherapy

LEARNING OBJECTIVES

Upon completion of Chapter 16, you should be able to answer the following questions.

1. How are insight and the therapist-patient relationship important in the psychodynamic approach to therapeutic change?

2. Describe three techniques psychodynamic psychotherapists use to bring about therapeutic change.

3. What are the similarities and differences between psychoanalysis and psychodynamic psychotherapy?

4. What are the four steps involved in systematic desensitization?

5. How does flooding differ from graded exposure?

6. What advantages does virtual reality exposure therapy offer over traditional graded exposure?

7. How does participatory modeling work to alleviate fear responses?

8. How is skills training useful in helping people with specific interpersonal deficits?

9. In what ways are Albert Ellis's Rational-Emotive Behavior Therapy and Aaron Beck's Cognitive Therapy similar?

10. What do the letters A, B, and C refer to in Albert Ellis's ABC theory of psychopathology?

11.   What are the key assumptions of Gestalt therapy?

12.   How is the *"empty chair technique"* used by Gestalt therapists?

13.   What are the key assumptions of Rogers's client-centered therapy?

14.   In what ways does group therapy differ from individual therapy? What are some advantages of group therapy approaches?

15.   What is the aim and focus of family therapy?

16.   Compare how family-systems therapists, psychodynamic therapists, behavior therapists and cognitive-behavior therapists approach marital therapy.

17.   Discuss two major ways in which some psychotherapists integrate multiple therapeutic perspectives.

18.   What psychotropic medication is effective with each of the following disorders? How does each medication work, and what are the drawbacks to its use?

        Psychosis

        Depression

        Bipolar disorder

        Anxiety

19.   For what disorders is electroconvulsive therapy (ECT) effective? What are the pros and cons to the use of ECT?

20.   How are lobotomies accomplished? What are the consequences of this procedure?

21.   How do efficacy studies and efficiency studies differ? Why are both needed to evaluate psychotherapy?

PART TWO: REVIEW AND LEARN
Key Terms, Fill-In Exercises, Application and Using What You Have Learned

Before doing the exercises below, review the information you learned in this chapter. Reread the work you did in part one of this study guide chapter, plus the interim summaries and end-of-chapter summary in your textbook. Review any problem areas. Once you feel comfortable with the material, do the following exercises without referring to your notes or textbook. If you have difficulty with a term or question, mark it and come back to it. When you have finished an exercise, go back to your notes and the textbook to find the answers to the questions that gave you difficulty. Finally, check your answers (key terms against the textbook and the rest against the answer key).

KEY TERMS

Insight _____

_____

Therapeutic alliance _____

_____

Free association _____

_____

Interpretation _____

_____

Resistance _____

_____

Transference _____

_____

Psychoanalysis _____

_____

Psychodynamic psychotherapy _____

_____

Cognitive-behavioral _____

_____

Behavioral analysis _____

_____

Systematic desensitization _____

_____

Exposure techniques _____

_____

Flooding _____

_____

Graded exposure _____

_____

Virtual reality exposure therapy _____

_____

Response prevention _____

_____

Participatory modeling _____

_____

Skills training _____

_____

Social skills training _____

_____

Cognitive therapy _____

_____

Automatic thoughts _____

_____

ABC theory of psychopathology _____

_____

Rational-emotive behavior therapy _____

_____

Humanistic therapies _____

_____

Gestalt therapy _____

_____

Empty-chair technique _____

_____

Client-centered therapy _____

_____

Unconditional positive regard _____

_____

Group therapy _____

_____

Group process _____

_____

Self-help group _____

_____

Family therapy _____

_____

Genogram _____

_____

Marital or couples therapy _____

_____

Negative reciprocity _____

_____

Psychotherapy integration _____

_____

Psychotropic medications _____

_____

Antipsychotic medications _____

_____

Tardive dyskinesia _____

_____

Antidepressant medications _____

_____

Tricyclic antidepressants_____

_____

MAO inhibitors _____

_____

Selective serotonin reuptake inhibitors (SSRIs) _____

_____

Lithium _____

_____

Benzodiazepines _____

_____

Electroconvulsive therapy (ECT) _____

_____

Psychosurgery _____

_____

Meta-analysis _____

_____

Common factors _____

_____

Efficacy studies _____

_____

Effectiveness studies _____

_____

FILL-IN EXERCISES

Fill in the word or words that best fit in the spaces below.

1.   Understanding one's own psychological processes is referred to as _____.

2.   In psychodynamic treatment, the patient has to feel comfortable enough with the therapist in order to speak about emotionally significant experiences, a phenomenon called the therapeutic _____.

3.   _____ _____ is a technique used in psychodynamic psychotherapies for exploring associational networks and unconscious processes involved in symptom formation. Using this technique, the therapist instructs the patient to say whatever comes to mind.

4.   A central technique of psychodynamic techniques is the _____ of conflicts, defenses, compromise-formations, and repetitive interpersonal patterns, whereby the therapist helps the person understand his or her experiences in a new light.

5.   _____ refers to barriers to free association or treatment that the patient creates.

6.   _____ refers to the process whereby people experience similar thoughts, feelings, fears, wishes, and conflicts in new relationships as they did in past relationships.

7.   The first kind of psychotherapy developed was _____, in which the patient lies on a couch and the analyst sits behind him or her.

8.   Cognitive-behavioral therapists begin with a careful _____ _____, examining the stimuli or thoughts that precede or are associated with a symptom.

9.   The procedure in which the patient gradually confronts a phobic stimulus mentally while in a relaxed state that inhibits anxiety is referred to as _____ _____.

10.   In the technique of _____, the patient confronts the phobic stimulus all at once. A modification of this procedure that involves presenting real stimuli that are increasingly intense is called _____ _____.

11.   A key component of all exposure techniques is _____ _____, which involves keeping the patient from acting in ways that allow avoidance of the feared stimulus.

12.   _____ _____ training is a behavioral procedure that has been devised for people with specific interpersonal deficits such as social awkwardness or lack of assertiveness.

13.   Aaron Beck refers to the things people spontaneously say to themselves and the assumptions they make as _____ thoughts.

14.   According to Albert Ellis, patients can rid themselves of unhappiness if they learn to maximize their _____ thinking and minimize their _____ thinking.

15.   The core of Beck's therapy, like that of Ellis, is challenging _____ distortions.

16.   To Gestalt therapists, understanding _____ one feels a certain way is far less important than recognizing _____ one feels that way.

17.   The *empty chair technique* is one of the best known procedures used by _____ therapists.

18.   Carl Rogers was among the first to refer to people who seek treatment as _____ rather than patients

19.   In Rogerian therapy, the therapist demonstrates unconditional _____ _____ for the patient, expressing an attitude of fundamental acceptance without any requirements or conditions.

20.   In group therapy, members of the group not only talk about problems in their own lives, but also gain from exploring a _____ _____, or the way members of the group interact with each other.

21.   One of the oldest and best known _____-_____ groups is Alcoholics Anonymous.

22.   As in group and psychodynamic therapy, the focus of family therapy is often on _____ as well as on content.

23.   Negative _____ refers to the tendency of members of a couple to respond to negative comments or actions by their partner with negative behaviors in return.

24.   Some therapists choose and combine techniques from different approaches to fit the particular case, a practice referred to as _____ therapy, one strategy of psychotherapy integration.

25.   The most serious side effect of antipsychotic medications is a movement disorder called _____ _____.

26.   Antidepressant medications increase the amount of the neurotransmitters_____ and/or _____ in the synapses and appear to reduce depression by correcting for depletion of these neurotransmitters.

27.   For bipolar disorder, _____ is the treatment of choice.

28.   Benzodiazepines work by increasing the activity of _____, a neurotransmitter that inhibits activation throughout the nervous system, thereby reducing anxiety.

29.   Electroconvulsive therapy (ECT) is currently used in the treatment of severe _____.

30.   _____ studies assess treatment outcomes under highly controlled conditions, while _____ studies assess treatment outcome under less controlled circumstances as practiced by clinicians in the field.

USING WHAT YOU HAVE LEARNED

Identify the type of therapy and/or approach associated with each of the following procedures.

1. A therapist places an empty chair in front of the patient and has him imagine his ex-girlfriend is in the chair. The patient tells her how he felt when she broke up with him.

2. A therapist works with a client to help him grow and mature, to help him experience himself as he really is. The therapist helps him identify feelings and offers him a supportive environment, expressing an attitude of fundamental acceptance without any strings attached.

3. A therapist trains a patient in deep relaxation. She then presents the patient with a hierarchically ordered sequence of stimuli that frighten him.

4. A therapist trains a patient to examine her irrational beliefs and the role they play in causing a negative emotional response. He demonstrates to the patient the illogic in her beliefs and then teaches her alternative ways of thinking.

5. A therapist works with the patient to develop a map of her family over four generations, looking for similarities between her current problems and problems in the family's past.

6. A patient visits his therapist 3 times a week. He lies on a couch, while she sits behind him. Often she instructs him to say whatever comes to mind -- thoughts, feelings, images, fantasies, memories, or wishes -- and to try to censor nothing.

APPLICATION

Situation

A friend of yours has been having a bad time with anxiety. She's been experiencing severe episodes of panic, accompanied by hyperventilation, a racing heart beat, and feelings of dizziness. When the attacks occur, she's petrified, feeling certain that she's having a stroke. She feels sure that she's going to have a panic attack while driving the car and that she'll pass out, lose control of the car and kill herself and someone else. She feels safe only if she stays at home or close enough to home that she can quickly return there if an attack occurs. She's always checking her pulse, looking for "signs" that a panic attack is about to happen. She decides to ask her doctor to refer her for help.

Questions to Answer

1. Based on what you've read in this chapter, what do you believe would be the most appropriate psychotherapeutic approach for her? Why?

2. How would a therapist using this approach conceptualize her problems?

3. What procedures would the therapist using this approach employ?

4. Regardless of what approach her therapist follows, what important characteristics should he or she display?

5. Suppose pharmacotherapy were recommended for her. What type of medication would likely be effective?

6. What would be some of the drawbacks associated with pharmacotherapy alone?

PART THREE: TEST AND KNOW
SAMPLE TEST QUESTIONS

Test how well you have learned this chapter's material by answering the sample test questions. You may wish to mark your answers on a separate sheet of paper so you can reuse this test for exam review. Once you have completed the exam, check your answers and then go back to your notes and the textbook to review questions you found difficult.

1. To bring about therapeutic change, psychodynamic psychotherapies rely on three techniques

   a.   empathy, interpretation, and analysis of transference
   b.   free association, interpretation, and collaborative empiricism
   c.   interpretation, response prevention, and unconditional positive regard
   d.   free association, interpretation, and analysis of transference

2.   Transference refers to

   a.   the process whereby people experience similar thoughts, feelings, fears, wishes, and conflicts in new relationships as they did in past relationships
   b.   the replacement of a conditioned fear response with relaxation in the process of systematic desensitization
   c.   how selective serotonin reuptake inhibitors (SSRIs) work at the synapse
   d.   the process by which the therapist models a desired behavior and gradually induces the patient to participate in it

3.   Although many therapists continue to practice behavior therapy (treatment based primarily on behaviorist learning principles), most who make use of learning principles today are _____ in their orientation.

   a.   humanistic   b.   structural and strategic
   c.   cognitive-behavioral   d.   eclectic

4.   The effectiveness of cognitive-behavioral therapies lies in their

   a.   ability to target highly specific psychological processes
   b.   use of empathy and unconditional positive regard
   c.   focus on the individual in the context of his or her family system
   d.   focus on helping the individual to express repressed feelings

5.   According to the cognitive-behavioral approach, phobic responses, like all avoidance responses, are

   a.   difficult to treat
   b.   particularly resistant to extinction
   c.   treatable by helping the patient gain insight into his or her own psychological processes
   d.   treatable through the use of active procedures such as the empty-chair technique

6.   A procedure in which the therapist demonstrates a behavior and then encourages the patient to engage in the same behavior is

   a.   social skills training   b.   graded exposure
   c.   participatory modeling   d.   counter-conditioning

7.   The "C" in Ellis's ABC theory of psychopathology refers to

   a.   belief systems
   b.   emotional consequences
   c.   activating conditions
   d.   unconscious conflicts

8.   Beck, like Ellis, views cognitive therapy as a process of _____ , in which patient and therapist work together testing hypotheses.

    a.   collaborative empiricism   b.   participatory modeling
    c.   interpretation   d.   growing and maturing

9.   The aim of humanistic therapies is to

    a.   help people understand the internal workings of their mind and thus gain the capacity to make conscious, rational, adult choices
    b.   change maladaptive behavior patterns
    c.   help people to a realization of the role their thoughts play in emotional or mental unhappiness, ineffectuality, and disturbance
    d.   help people get in touch with their feelings, with their "true selves," and with a sense of meaning in life

10.   One of the most widely practiced humanistic therapies is

    a.   the structural and strategic approach
    b.   rational-emotive therapy
    c.   family-systems therapy
    d.   client-centered therapy

11.   In Rogerian therapy, the therapist creates a supportive atmosphere by demonstrating _____ .

    a.   love and respect for the client
    b.   a therapeutic alliance with the client
    c.   unconditional positive regard for the client
    d.   collaborative empiricism to the client

12.   Losing touch with one's emotions and one's authentic "inner" voice leads to psychological problems such as depression and anxiety, according to

    a.   Ellis's ABC theory of psychopathology
    b.   Gestalt therapy
    c.   Rogers's client-centered therapy
    d.   the Consumer Reports survey

13.   Self-help groups differ from other forms of group therapy in that they

    a.   are generally not guided by a professional
    b.   focus on a common issue or disorder
    c.   are insight-oriented rather than behaviorally-oriented
    d.   reduce the problem of transference as there is no leader

14. One of the most important contributions of Paul Wachtel's integrative approach is the notion that people's fears and expectations create self-reinforcing behaviors that often lead them to get precisely what they fear. This concept is known as:

     a. negative reciprocity   b. learned helplessness
     c. cyclical psychodynamics   d. response prevention

15. Antipsychotic medications are also sometimes called

     a. benzodiazepines
     b. selective serotonin reuptake inhibitors (SSRIs)
     c. monoamine oxidase (MAO) inhibitors
     d. major tranquilizers

16. Antipsychotic medications inhibit the action of

     a. monoamine oxidase   b. dopamine
     c. serotonin   d. norepinephrine

17. Tricyclic antidepressants

     a. block reuptake of serotonin and norepinephrine into the presynaptic membrane
     b. keep the chemical monoamine oxidase from breaking down neurotransmitter substances in the presynaptic neuron, making more neurotransmitter available for release into the synapse
     c. target serotonin rather than norepinephrine
     d. are the treatment of choice for bipolar disorder

18. Fluoxetine (Prozac) is the best known

     a. benzodiazepine
     b. antipsychotic
     c. selective serotonin reuptake inhibitor
     d. benzodiazepine

19. The main side effect of electroconvulsive therapy (ECT) is

     a. loss of sexual desire   b. memory loss
     c. dry mouth, restlessness, agitation   d. weight gain, nausea, light-headedness

20. ECT can sometimes be useful in treating _____, as well as depression.

     a. anorexia   b. schizophrenia
     c. antisocial personality disorder   d. mania

ANSWERS

FILL-IN EXERCISES

1. insight 2. alliance 3. free association 4. interpretation 5. resistance 6. transference 7. psychoanalysis
8. behavioral analysis 9. systematic desensitization 10. flooding; graded exposure 11. response prevention
12. social skills 13. automatic 14. rational; irrational 15. cognitive   16. why; that 17. Gestalt 18. clients
19. positive regard 20. group process 21. self-help 22. process 23. reciprocity 24. eclectic 25. tardive
dyskinesia 26. norepinephrine, serotonin 27. lithium 28. GABA 29. depression 30. efficacy, effectiveness

USING WHAT YOU HAVE LEARNED

1. empty chair technique (Gestalt therapy, humanistic approaches)
2. client-centered therapy (humanistic approaches)
3. systematic desensitization (behavior therapy)
4. rational-emotive behavior therapy (cognitive therapy)
5. family therapy (genogram)
6. psychoanalysis (psychodynamic approaches)

APPLICATION

1. Cognitive-behavior therapy. Its effectiveness for anxiety is well established.
2. Panic attacks are the result of associating autonomic reactions with an impending panic attack, leading to panic whenever these reactions occur. Feelings of helplessness in the face of an impending attack, and catastrophic thoughts about consequences compound the problem. Staying at home is the result of avoidance learning.
3. Paced breathing exercises; repeated exposure to experience of racing heart; rational analysis of the accuracy of catastrophic beliefs.
4. Empathy; warm therapist-client relationship; instilling a sense of hope and efficacy.
5. Benzodiazepines or antidepressants.
6. Possible physiological or psychological dependency.

SAMPLE TEST QUESTIONS

1.	d	11.	c
2.	a	12.	b
3.	c	13.	a
4.	a	14.	c
5.	b	15.	d
6.	c	16.	b
7.	b	17.	a
8.	a	18.	c
9.	d	19.	b
10.	d	20.	d

Chapter 17
Social Cognition

PART ONE: PRE-READ AND WORK
Outline and Learning Objectives

Pre-read this chapter's table of contents and end-of-chapter summary. Then, use the outline segment-by-segment to help you work through the chapter. Jot down your own questions, comments, and notes in the space provided. Make a note of difficult areas that you will need to review (include page numbers). Then, answer the questions in the learning objectives section that follows. Check off those you are confident that you can answer well. Re-read the material in the text for the questions about which you are less confident. Record the important points from your reading in the space below each question.

OUTLINE

Social Cognition

Perceiving Other People

Stereotypes and Prejudice

Attribution

Biases in Social Information Processing

Applications

Social and Nonsocial Cognition-like Applications

Attitudes

The Nature of Attitudes

Attitudes and Behavior

Persuasion

Cognitive Dissonance

The Self

Self-Esteem

Self-Consistency

Self-Presentation

From Brain to Behavior: Physical Health and Views of the Self

A Global Vista: Culture and Self

LEARNING OBJECTIVES

Upon completion of Chapter 17, you should be able to answer the following questions.

1.   Describe several different cognitive models of how information is represented in long-term memory that have guided research on social cognition.

2.   In what ways does attractiveness influence first impressions?

3.   What is the role of schemas in the processing of social information?

4.   How do stereotypes lead to prejudice?

5.   How does the notion of the authoritarian personality explain prejudice?

6.   What is implicit racism, and how does this differ from a person's explicit attitudes?

7.   How does prejudice result from ingroup-outgroup distinctions?

8.   Why is contact alone insufficient to reduce intergroup hostility?

9.   What three types of information do people rely on when making attributions for behavior?

10.   How do discounting and augmentation influence attributions?

11.   What are the implications of a positive or negative attributional style?

12.   What is the correspondence bias and how does it influence attributions?

13.   How do self-serving biases affect people's evaluations of themselves?

14.   How do cognitive and motivational biases result in faulty processing of social information?

15.   In what major ways does social cognition differ from nonsocial cognition?

16.   What is an attitude and what are the three components of an attitude that some psychologists distinguish?

17.   Differentiate between attitude strength and attitude accessibility.

18.   Explain what is meant by the following dimensions of attitudes: cognitive complexity, attitudinal ambivalence, and attitudinal coherence.

19.   Why aren't attitudes strongly predictive of behavior?

20.   Discuss each of the following components of persuasion distinguished by psychologists: source, message, channel, context, receiver.

21.   Under what circumstances are the central and the peripheral routes to persuasion more persuasive, according to the elaboration likelihood model?

22.   What is the phenomenon of cognitive dissonance?

23.   How do perception of choice and size of rewards and punishments influence the extent to which cognitive dissonance arises?

24.   Explain each of the following phenomena associated with cognitive dissonance:

Postdecision regret

Postdecision dissonance reduction

Effort justification

25.   How do *self-perception theory* and *self-presentation* account for the phenomenon of cognitive dissonance?

26.   Can it be said that cognitive dissonance is a culturally universal phenomenon?

27.   How are the notions of *self-concept* and *self-esteem* related to the concept of *self*?

28.   What are some common ways that people use to maintain and even enhance their self-esteem?

29.   How are the motives of *self-consistency* and *self-esteem* related?

30.   Explain how the process of *self-presentation* or *impression management* can influence an individual's behavior.

31.   What are the emotional and physical consequences of discrepancies between (a) *actual self* and *ideal self* and (b) *actual self* and *ought self?*

32.   How can the concept of "self" be considered culturally relative?

PART TWO: REVIEW AND LEARN
Key Terms, Fill-In Exercises, Application and Using What You Have Learned

Before doing the exercises below, review the information you learned in this chapter. Reread the work you did in part one of this study guide chapter, plus the interim summaries and end-of-chapter summary in your textbook. Review any problem areas. Once you feel comfortable with the material, do the following exercises without referring to your notes or textbook. If you have difficulty with a term or question, mark it and come back to it. When you have finished an exercise, go back to your notes and the textbook to find the answers to the questions that gave you difficulty. Finally, check your answers (key terms against the textbook and the rest against the answer key).

KEY TERMS

Upon completion of Chapter 17, you should be able to define the following terms.

Social psychology   _____

_____

Social cognition _____

_____

First impressions   _____

_____

Halo effect   _____

_____

Stereotypes   _____

_____

Prejudice   _____

_____

Discrimination   _____

_____

Authoritarian personality _____

_____

Ingroups   _____

_____

Outgroups   _____

_____

Social identity theory   _____

_____

Superordinate goals   _____

_____

Attribution   _____

_____

Intuitive scientist   _____

_____

External attribution

_____

_____

Internal attribution

_____

_____

Consensus

_____

_____

Consistency

_____

_____

Distinctiveness

_____

_____

Discounting

_____

_____

Augmentation

_____

_____

Attributional style

_____

_____

Correspondence bias

_____

_____

Self-serving bias

_____

_____

Attitude _____

_____

Attitude strength_____

_____

Attitude importance   _____

_____

Attitude accessibility   _____

_____

Implicit attitudes_____

_____

Attitudinal ambivalence   _____

_____

Attitudinal coherence   _____

_____

Persuasion   _____

_____

Attitude inoculation   _____

_____

Central route   _____

_____

Peripheral route_____

_____

Elaboration likelihood model   _____

_____

Cognitive dissonance _____

_____

Self-perception theory _____

_____

Self _____

_____

Self-concept _____

_____

Self-esteem _____

_____

Self-handicapping _____

_____

Self-consistency _____

_____

Self-presentation _____

_____

Self-presentational predicaments _____

_____

Self-monitoring _____

_____

Actual self _____

_____

Ideal self   _____

_____

Ought self   _____

_____

FILL-IN EXERCISES

Fill in the word or words that best fit in the spaces below.

1.   Social _____ refers to the processes by which people make sense out of themselves, others, social interactions, and relationships.

2.   People's tendency to assume that positive qualities cluster together is a phenomenon referred to as the _____ effect.

3.   _____ are characteristics attributed to people based on their membership in specific groups.

4.   _____ involves one's thoughts or opinions about another person or group, based on stereotypes. _____ refers to behaviors that follow from negative evaluations or attitudes towards members of particular groups.

5.   Adorno and his colleagues identified what they called the _____ _____, characterized by a tendency to hate people who are different or downtrodden.

6.   Prejudice requires a distinction between _____ and _____, that is, people who belong to the group and those who do not.

7.   People tend to perceive members of _____ as much more homogeneous than they really are and to emphasize the individuality of _____ members.

8.   Social identity theory suggests that people derive part of their identity from the _____ to which they belong.

9.   The process of inferring the causes of one's own and others' mental states and behaviors is referred to as _____.

10.   According to one view, when people make attributions they are like intuitive _____: They rely on intuitive theories, frame hypotheses, collect data about themselves and others, and draw conclusions as best they can based on the pattern of data they have observed.

11.   Understanding people's behavior may involve _____ attributions -- attributing behavior to the demands of the situation in which is occurred, or _____ attributions -- attributing behavior to aspects of a person's personality, or may involve a combination of the two.

12.   The extent to which a person always responds in the same way to the same stimulus, referred to as _____, is one of three types of information that are important in attribution judgments. The other two types of information are _____ and _____.

13.   Increasing an internal attribution for behavior, despite situational demands, is referred to as _____.

14.   A person's habitual manner of assigning causes to behaviors or events is referred to as _____ _____.

15.   _____ bias refers to the tendency to assume that other people's behavior corresponds to their internal states rather than external situations.

16.   _____ bias refers to people's tendency to see themselves in a more positive light than others see them.

17.   The statement "alcohol leads to major social problems" is an example of the _____ component of an attitude.

18.   Attitude _____ refers to the personal relevance of an attitude and the psychological significance of that attitude for an individual. Attitude _____ refers to the ease with which an attitude comes to mind. Both can affect an attitude's strength.

19.   _____ attitudes involve associations between attitude objects and feelings that regulate thought and behavior unconsciously and automatically.

20.   Attitudinal _____ refers to the extent to which a given attitude object is associated with conflicting evaluative responses.

21.   The extent to which an attitude is internally consistent is referred to as attitudinal _____.

22.   Deliberate efforts to change an attitude are referred to as _____.

23.   Building up an individual's resistance to persuasion, by presenting weak arguments that are easily countered is referred to as _____ _____.

24.   According to the elaboration likelihood model, _____ appeals to persuasion are more effective when the person both is motivated to think about a topic and has the time to consider the arguments.

25.   _____ _____ occurs when a person experiences a discrepancy between an attitude and a behavior, or between an attitude and a new piece of information.

26.   _____-_____ theory holds that individuals infer their attitudes, emotions, and other internal states by observing their own behavior.

27.   Self-_____ refers to people's self evaluation -- how much they like and respect themselves.

28.   The process by which people may set themselves up to fail when success is uncertain in order to preserve their self-esteem is referred to as _____-_____.

29.   The process by which people attempt to control the impressions that others form of them is called _____-_____.

30.   Individual differences in the degree to which people manage their impressions are referred to as self-_____.

31.   Hopes, aspirations, and wishes that define the way a person would like to be, make up the _____ _____.

APPLICATION

Situation

Ms. Beagley is having some problems in her grade-7 class. Two cliques of girls have formed. These cliques have become increasingly hostile toward one another, with taunting, name calling, and verbal aggression on the rise. In her attempt to solve the problem, Ms. Beagley has rearranged the seating in her classroom, so that girls from different cliques must be seatmates. So far, this hasn't worked. Instead, hostilities seem to have increased. When one girl accidentally spilled her seatmate's coke at lunch, she was immediately accused of doing it on purpose. "You and all your friends are the same. You're jerks!" she was told by her seatmate. When the same girl offered her science book to her seatmate who had forgotten hers, her seatmate's response was, "What choice did she have, teacher would've made her loan it to me anyway!" Ms. Beagley cannot figure out what is happening in her class. She calls upon you to help her understand why these girls are so antagonistic to one another and to brainstorm with her for ways to solve this problem.

Questions to Answer

1. From what you've read in Chapter 17, what do you think is going on in Ms. Beagley's class?

2. What process do you think is at the root of the hostility and discrimination between these two groups of girls?

3. What kind of errors or overgeneralizations can you see in how the girls in one clique view those in the other? How would you expect them to interpret positive and negative actions performed by members of their clique? How would they interpret the same behaviors performed by members of the other clique?

4. Why hasn't Ms. Beagley's strategy of rearranging the seating plan been successful in resolving the hostilities? What would be a better way to reduce hostilities between the groups of girls?

Using What You Have Learned

Provide the correct label for the phenomena described in each of the following:

1.   Joanne is an extremely attractive woman. She is a tall, slim, well-dressed business woman. When they first meet her, most people automatically assume that she must be competent and confident.

2.   Bill's car broke down at a busy intersection. As he sat there helplessly, motorists behind him began honking and shouting things at him like: "You jerk, why are you trying to hold up all the traffic?" "What's your problem? Do you enjoy making people late for work?"

3.   After hearing a vignette about a criminal attorney, most subjects recalled that he was shrewd and calculating, but few remembered the color of his briefcase.

4.   Hearing about the success of a gifted musician, whose father was also a very successful musician, one individual argued: "Oh well, she didn't have to work at it very hard. She's riding on her father's coat tails."

5.   Steve had to choose between psychology and dentistry. It was tough. He thought about it for a long time and then chose psychology. Afterward, he was told that dentists make a lot more money, and he began to ruminate about his choice. Then, he came across an article on the high incidence of stress-related illness in dentists. To ease his mind about his choice of psychology, he began reading all he could find about the stress dentists are under.

PART THREE: TEST AND KNOW
SAMPLE TEST QUESTIONS

Test how well you have learned this chapter's material by answering the sample test questions. You may wish to mark your answers on a separate sheet of paper so you can reuse this test for exam review. Once you have completed the exam, check your answers and then go back to your notes and the textbook to review questions you found difficult.

1.   Jacob is an accountant with a busy practice. He is tall and athletic. Just seeing him pass by on the street, people "know" he's a good accountant. This inference people make about Jacob's abilities is known as a

    a.   self-serving bias   b.   halo effect
    c.   correspondence bias   d.   stereotype

2.   When Julie heard that her doctor was a champion motocross rider, she just couldn't believe it. But, when she checked and found out it was true, she never forgot it. Motocross riding just does not fit in her _____ about doctors.

    a.   attributions   b.   prejudice
    c.   schema   d.   implicit attitude

3.   Schemas about the personal attributes of a group of people that are often overgeneralized, inaccurate, and resistant to new information are referred to as

    a.   implicit racism   b.   stereotypes
    c.   discrimination   d.   prejudice

4.   The _____ personality refers to a particular personality style that is prone to hate people who are different or downtrodden.

    a.   antisocial   b.   authoritative
    c.   borderline   d.   authoritarian

5.   Jane Elliot's classroom study in which she informed children that brown-eyed children are superior and blue-eyed children are inferior clearly demonstrated how

    a.   a distinction between ingroups and outgroups leads to prejudice
    b.   schemas can be altered easily by simply presenting information that conflicts with the content of the schema
    c.   cognitive dissonance plays a major role in even the attitudes of school children
    d.   children are resistant to information that they know is wrong, even when it's presented by an adult authority figure

6. A study of how Hindu and Muslim students in Bangladesh explained the causes of helpful or unhelpful behavior presented in vignettes revealed which of the following?

    a. Helpful acts by ingroup members were attributed to environmental circumstances.
    b. Helpful acts by outgroup members were seen to reflect enduring personality attributes.
    c. Unhelpful acts by outgroup members were attributed to environmental circumstance.
    d. Helpful acts by ingroup members were seen to reflect enduring personality attributes.

7. The study of the conflict between the Rattlers and Eagles groups at a Boy Scout summer camp showed that

    a. cooperation and contact between the two groups were required to reduce conflict.
    b. extended contact between the two groups (i.e., bringing the two groups together for pleasant activities) was what was required to reduce conflict.
    c. there was nothing that could reduce conflict between the two groups.
    d. conflict between the two groups could only be reduced by terminating the camp.

8. In making attributions to the person or to the situation, people rely on which of the following types of information?

    a. stereotypes, ingroups, outgroups
    b. consensus, consistency, distinctiveness
    c. cause, effect, correlation
    d. discounting, augmenting, attributing

9. "I know what Jerry said to you was mean" said Phil, "but, let's give him a break. He just found out he failed all his midterms." Phil's attribution for Jerry's behavior shows evidence of

    a. consensus   b. augmentation
    c. discounting   d. consistency

10. Correspondence bias refers to

    a. looking for information that fits with the way a person already views him/herself
    b. the effects of first impressions on our judgments of people
    c. the tendency to attribute behaviors to people's personalities and to ignore possible situational causes
    d. the belief people hold that positive qualities tend to cluster together

11. A majority of people rate themselves above average on most dimensions. This is, of course, statistically impossible, and is a good example of:

    a. self-consistency   b. correspondence bias
    c. augmentation   d. self-serving bias

12.   Social psychologists distinguish the following three components of an attitude

    a.   cognitive, evaluative, behavioral
    b.   conscious, unconscious, preconscious
    c.   cognitive, social, physical
    d.   consensus, consistency, distinctiveness

13.   The best form of persuasion when an attitude is not strongly held and is based on minimal knowledge is to

    a.   encourage emotional responses that bypass the belief components of the attitude
    b.   induce the person to think carefully and weigh the arguments
    c.   overwhelm the person with so much information that he or she no longer even knows what the issue is
    d.   offer tangible incentives to the person to change her opinion

14.   Which of the following characteristics of a speaker play an important role in how successful her attempt at persuasion will be?

    a.   credibility
    b.   attractiveness
    c.   power
    d.   all of the above

15.   In Ms. Jones' grade 6 class, the students have been discussing peer pressure and cigarette smoking. Ms. Jones has presented weak arguments in favor of smoking – "smoking is cool," "it will make you seem like an adult," and "it will make you more attractive to the opposite sex," and so on. The students then work in groups to develop counterarguments against these ideas. This method of developing resistance to peer pressure to begin smoking is referred to as:

    a.   effort justification
    b.   self-handicapping
    c.   attitude inoculation
    d.   elaboration likelihood

16.   After Bill bought his new Mac computer, he came across an ad for a Dell that had all the features he wanted and cost less. Bill began to collect all the information he could find on the value of buying a Mac. Bill's behavior was motivated by

    a.   elaboration likelihood
    b.   cognitive dissonance
    c.   self-handicapping
    d.   attitude inoculation

17.   Self-consistency refers to

    a.   people's tendency to perceive themselves in a manner consistent with the view of those around them

    b.   the ability to achieve a balance between the real, ideal, and ought selves

    c.   people's tendency to behave in a consistent manner across a variety of situations

    d.   people's tendency to interpret information to fit the way they see themselves and to prefer people who verify their view of themselves

18.   Stephanie grew up in a home that placed a lot of value on academic success. She has always felt that her self-worth was linked to accomplishments at school, but since starting college she's not so sure she's smart enough to live up to her parents' high expectations. Lately, her actions have puzzled her roommates, as it seems like she's been setting herself up to fail. Rather than spending her time studying for her finals, Stephanie has been partying every night. What is the most likely explanation for her behavior?

    a.   impression management, to control her parents' views of her abilities

    b.   self-handicapping, to preserve her self esteem

    c.   self-consistency, to interpret information to fit her uncertain view of herself

    d.   attitude inoculation, to prepare her parents for her eventual failure

19.   Self-presentational predicaments, in which our desires to influence the impressions other people form of us fail, are most frequently associated with the emotional response of:.

    a.   embarrassment

    b.   fear

    c.   guilt

    d.   resentment

20.   Emotions, such as fear, guilt, uneasiness, and self-contempt, which characterize anxious individuals, may be the result of a discrepancy between

    a.   ideal self and ought self

    b.   actual self and ideal self

    c.   actual self and ought self

    d.   self as subject and self as object

ANSWERS

FILL-IN EXERCISES

1. cognition 2. halo 3. stereotypes 4. prejudice; discrimination 5. authoritarian personality 6. ingroups, outgroups 7. outgroups; ingroup 8. groups 9. attribution 10. scientists 11. external; internal
12. consistency; consensus, distinctiveness 13. augmentation 14. attributional style 15. correspondence
16. self-serving 17. cognitive 18. importance; accessibility 19. implicit 20. ambivalence 21. coherence
22. persuasion 23. attitude inoculation 24. rational 25. cognitive dissonance 26. self-perception
27. esteem 28. self-handicapping 29 self-presentation (or impression management) 30. monitoring
31. ideal self

APPLICATION

1. Intergroup antagonism and prejudice
2. Ingroup-outgroup distinction
3. They perceive members of the outgroup as much more homogeneous than they really are. They make the following attribution errors in explaining the behavior of outgroup members: When considering the behavior of those not in their clique (i.e., outgroup members) the girls attribute positive behavior (one girl offering to share her book) to environmental circumstances and negative behavior (spilling the coke) to internal personality attributes. Most likely they would attribute positive and negative behaviors performed by *ingroup* members to internal and external causes, respectively.
4. As was the case in the study with the Rattlers and Eagles at a boy scout camp, contact alone is not enough to resolve conflict. The contact must also involve cooperation. Ms. Beagley should create a situation that involves superordinate goals that require the two groups to cooperate for the benefit of all.

USING WHAT YOU HAVE LEARNED

1. halo effect 2. correspondence bias 3. schema 4. discounting 5. cognitive dissonance (postdecision dissonance reduction)

SAMPLE TEST QUESTIONS

1.	b	11.	d
2.	c	12.	a
3.	b	13.	a
4.	d	14.	d
5.	a	15.	c
6.	d	16.	b
7.	a	17.	d
8.	b	18.	b
9.	c	19.	a
10.	c	20.	c

Chapter 18
Interpersonal Processes

PART ONE: PRE-READ AND WORK
Outline and Learning Objectives

Pre-read this chapter's table of contents and end-of-chapter summary. Then, use the outline segment-by-segment to help you work through the chapter. Jot down your own questions, comments, and notes in the space provided. Make a note of key terms and of difficult areas that you will need to review (include page numbers). Then, answer the questions in the learning objectives section that follows. Check off those you are confident that you can answer well. Re-read the material in the text for the questions about which you are less confident. Record the important points from your reading in the space below each question.

OUTLINE

Relationships

Factors Leading to Interpersonal Attraction

Love

A Global Vista: Love in Cross-Cultural Perspective

The Dark Side of Relationships

Altruism

Theories of Altruism

Bystander Intervention

Aggression

Violence and Culture

Violence and Gender

The Roots of Violence

From Brain to Behavior: Biological Foundations of Aggression

Social Influence

Obedience

Conformity

Group Processes

Everyday Social Influence

Individuals, Groups, and the Nature of Human Nature

LEARNING OBJECTIVES

Upon completion of Chapter 18, you should be able to answer the following questions.

1. How does each of the following factors influence interpersonal attraction?

    Proximity

    Interpersonal rewards

    Similarity

    Physical attractiveness

2. What are the differences between passionate love and companionate love?

3. What are the differences in "sexual strategies" of males and females, as described by evolutionary psychologists?

4. How do attachment theorists view romantic love?

5. How do the concepts of love and marriage differ across cultures?

6. What are some of the characteristics of people in stable, long-term relationships?

7. How does the notion of ethical hedonism explain altruism?

8.   What do evolutionary psychologists mean by reciprocal altruism?

9.   How does the presence of others influence bystander intervention?

10.   How do the prevalence and form of aggression vary by culture and gender?

11.   What are the similarities and differences between the instinctual and evolutionary views of aggression?

12.   What neural and hormonal systems have been found to underlie aggressive behavior?

13.   How does frustration lead to aggression? What environmental factors have been found to increase both aggression and frustration?

14.   How do television violence and pornography affect aggression?

15.   How does the General Aggression Model (GAM) explain aggression?

16.   What factors influence obedience, according to Milgram's research?

17.   How did Solomon Asch demonstrate the power of conformity?

18.   How do culture and gender relate to conformity?

19.   How do reference groups influence the norms to which people respond?

20.   How can people's attitudes and behavior be influenced by the roles they assume?

21.   What are several different roles that commonly emerge in groups?

22.   How is the performance of group members influenced by the presence of other group members?

23.   How do the following three leadership styles differ: autocratic, democratic, and laissez-faire?

24.   Describe the leadership dimensions of task orientation and relationship organization.

25.   Explain how the principles of reciprocity and commitment operate in everyday social influence.

PART TWO: REVIEW AND LEARN
Key Terms, Fill-In Exercises, Application and Using What You Have Learned

Before doing the exercises below, review the information you learned in this chapter. Reread the work you did in part one of this study guide chapter, plus the interim summaries and end-of-chapter summary in your textbook. Review any problem areas. Once you feel comfortable with the material, do the following exercises without referring to your notes or textbook. If you have difficulty with a term or question, mark it and come back to it. When you have finished an exercise, go back to your notes and the textbook to find the answers to the questions that gave you difficulty. Finally, check your answers (key terms against the textbook and the rest against the answer key).

KEY TERMS

Altruism   _____

_____

Situational variables   _____

_____

Dispositional variables   _____

_____

Need to belong   _____

_____

Interpersonal attraction   _____

_____

Social exchange theories   _____

_____

Matching hypothesis   _____

_____

Passionate love _____

_____

Companionate love _____

_____

Sexual strategies _____

_____

Ethical hedonism _____

_____

Reciprocal altruism _____

_____

Bystander intervention _____

_____

Diffusion of responsibility _____

_____

Aggression _____

_____

Hostile aggression _____

_____

Instrumental aggression _____

_____

Frustration-aggression hypothesis _____

_____

Social influence _____

_____

Self-fulfilling prophecies _____

_____

Obedience   _____

_____

Conformity   _____

_____

Group _____

_____

Norms _____

_____

Reference groups   _____

_____

Role   _____

_____

Task (or instrumental) leader   _____

_____

Social-emotional leader _____

_____

Social facilitation   _____

_____

Social loafing _____

_____

Leaders _____

_____

Door-in-the-face technique _____

_____

Foot-in-the-door technique _____

_____

Low-balling _____

_____

FILL-IN EXERCISES

Fill in the word or words that best fit in the spaces below.

1.   Helping another person with no apparent gain to oneself is referred to as _____.

2.   Social exchange theories hold that the foundation of relationships is _____ reward.

3.   In choosing partners, people tend to follow the _____ hypothesis, selecting partners they perceive to be equally attractive as themselves, not necessarily the most beautiful or handsome.

4.   Whereas _____ love is marked by intense physiological arousal and absorption in another person, _____ love involves deep affection, friendship, and emotional intimacy.

5.   According to evolutionary psychologists, short-term and long-term mating strategies are similar for _____ (males/females).

6.   _____ _____ refers to the doctrine that all behavior, no matter how apparently altruistic, is designed to increase one's own pleasure or reduce one's own pain.

7.   _____ _____ holds that natural selection favors animals that behave altruistically if the likely benefit to each individual over time exceeds the likely cost.

8.   "_____ *of responsibility*" refers to a diminished sense of personal responsibility to act because others are seen as equally responsible.

9.   Calm, pragmatic aggression is referred to as _____ aggression.

10.   Electrical stimulation of the lateral _____ results in attack behavior in cats or rhesus monkeys.

11.   Studies with rats find that the amount of aggressive behavior displayed by both sexes correlates with circulating blood _____ levels.

12.   Recent thinking suggests that frustration leads to aggression, to the extent that a frustrating event elicits an _____ emotion.

13.   Within countries as diverse as Spain, Italy, France, and the United States, the southern regions typically have the highest rates of _____ crime.

14.   Although viewing pornography does not _____ sexual violence, viewing pornographic *aggression* does appear to _____ men to the brutality of sexual violence.

15.   Although most people assume that low self-esteem is more closely allied with aggression than high self-esteem this assumption is incorrect. People with _____ high self-esteem behave more aggressively when their sense of self is threatened with negative evaluations.

16.   Social _____ refers to the effects of the presence of others on the way people think, feel, and behave

17.   Milgram's research reveals that people will obey, without limitations of conscience, if they believe an order comes from a legitimate _____.

18.   Solomon Asch's research demonstrated the powerful influence of _____.

19.   Groups whose norms matter to an individual, and hence have an impact on the individual's behavior, are known as _____ groups.

20.   A _____ is a position in a group that has norms specifying appropriate behavior for its occupants.

21.   The _____ _____ is the group member who takes responsibility for seeing that the group completes its tasks.

22.   The presence of other people can either help or hurt individual performance, a process called social _____.

23.   The process by which people exert less effort when is a group is referred to as social _____.

24. In Kurt Lewin's study where groups of boys made crafts after school, the style of leadership that led to neither satisfaction nor efficiency was a _____ style.

25. _____-_____ entails getting a commitment to a request and then changing the conditions of the request.

APPLICATION

Situation

Jan is a 10th grader who has just moved to a new school, midway through the term. She immediately strikes up a friendship with Ruth, the girl whose locker is beside hers. Ruth doesn't appear to have many friends and seems to really enjoy Jan's company. During her first week at the new school, Jan had lunch with Ruth every day. As she gets to know the other girls, however, Jan discovers that nobody likes Ruth. Everyone agrees that it's not cool to be seen with Ruth, although nobody really knows why. As Jan feels more and more comfortable with her new classmates, she feels more and more pressure to reject Ruth. Sitting with some of her classmates one day, the conversation turns to Ruth. All the other girls agree that she's a "loser." Someone then asks Jan what she thinks about Ruth. She wants to stand up for Ruth, yet at the same time, she wants to be accepted by her new classmates. So she agrees that Ruth is a loser.[*]

Questions to Answer

1. What is the phenomenon underlying Jan's dilemma?

2. What factors lead to Jan's agreeing with the opinion of the group, despite her personal feelings to the contrary?

3. Would it make any difference if another classmate had stood up for Ruth before they asked Jan what she thought?

4. What is the term that would describe the unspoken rule among the girls in Jan's class that it's not cool to be seen with Ruth?

5. Why would this group of girls be labeled a *positive* reference group for Jan in view of their behavior?

---

[*] *This situation was derived from Hanna, J. & Younger, A. (1991, April). Peer rejection and conformity. Paper presented at the biennial meeting of the Society for Research in Child Development, Seattle, WA.*

USING WHAT YOU HAVE LEARNED

You have been asked to write a short article for the college newspaper on the topic of love and romance. The article is intended to dispel common myths and to present a psychological perspective on the topic. The editors want you to focus on the following points. Based on what you've read in Chapter 18, what would you say on each of these topics?

1.   What is it that attracts couples to each other?

2.   How important is physical attractiveness for love and romance?

3.   Are there different kinds of love?

4.   Are men and women looking for the same things in romance?

5.   How important is romance to marriage?

PART THREE: TEST AND KNOW
SAMPLE TEST QUESTIONS

Test how well you have learned this chapter's material by answering the sample test questions. You may wish to mark your answers on a separate sheet of paper so you can reuse this test for exam review. Once you have completed the exam, check your answers and then go back to your notes and the textbook to review questions you found difficult.

1.   Proximity, similarity, attractiveness, and degree to which an interaction is rewarding are factors that influence

   a.   interpersonal attraction
   b.   altruism
   c.   frustration, and, hence, influence aggression
   d.   leadership

2.   _____ is high at the beginning of a relationship, but tends to diminish over time, with periodic resurges or "peaks." On the other hand, _____ usually grows over time through shared experience.

   a.   intimate love; passionate love
   b.   passionate love; companionate love
   c.   physical love; emotional love
   d.   romantic love; compassionate love

3. Attachment theorists argue that

    a.   insecurely attached infants will never be able to develop adult romantic relationships

    b.   while secure attachment in infancy is predictive of secure romantic relationships in adulthood, nothing can be predicted from insecure attachment relationships

    c.   adult romantic relationships are *not* related to mother-infant attachment

    d.   people pattern their romantic relationships on the mental models they constructed of earlier attachment relationships

4. The notion that all behavior, no matter how altruistic it appears to be, is designed to increase one's own pleasure or reduce one's own pain is referred to as

    a.   ethical hedonism

    b.   reciprocal altruism

    c.   diffusion of responsibility

    d.   instrumental altruism

5. Darley and Latane developed a multi-stage model of the decision-making process underlying bystander intervention. During stage 3, the presence of others

    a.   serves as an informational source (i.e., "is there a crisis here or isn't there?")

    b.   serves as a source of reassurance

    c.   serves to increase empathic distress in the bystander

    d.   leads to a diffusion of responsibility

6. Most contemporary psychodynamic psychologists view aggression as

    a.   a basic instinct in humans

    b.   a class of behaviors that societies implant

    c.   an inborn behavioral potential usually activated by frustration and anger

    d.   behavior that is pleasurable only to sadists, delinquents, and antisocial personalities

7. Across species, overt female aggression is largely elicited by

    a.   the mating attempts of a male when the female is unreceptive

    b.   competition between females for the same male

    c.   intrusion into their territory by another female

    d.   attacks on their young

8. A number of studies have implicated low levels of _____ in aggression.

    a.   testosterone

    b.   serotonin

    c.   adrenaline

    d.   blood sugar

9.   Electrical stimulation of the _____ can result in aggression and hostility in humans.

        a.   gonads   b.   hippocampus
        c.   amygdala   d.   cerebellum

10.   Dollard and Miller proposed that

        a.   When people become frustrated they become aggressive.
        b.   Aggression is one expression of conformity to a perceived social norm.
        c.   Aggression is more likely among people with unstable high self-esteem.
        d.   Aggression is more likely among men who feel they have been "dissed" – treated with
                perceived disrespect.

11.   Violent crimes such as rape, assault, murder, as well as prison unrest peak

        a.   during the spring because of the increase in testosterone levels in men
        b.   during the summer months when it is hot
        c.   during the fall when the imminent onset of winter leads to frustration
        d.   during the winter when daylight hours are shortest

12.   Which of the following is likely *not* a result of watching violent television programs?

        a.   increased arousal
        b.   increased inhibition
        c.   exposure to aggressive models
        d.   desensitization to violence

13.   In Milgram's research which of the following led to a *decrease* in obedience?

        a.   the presence of confederates who gave incorrect answers
        b.   moving the experimenter to the same room as the subject.
        c.   moving the victim into the same room as the subject
        d.   all of the above

14.   In Asch's research where subjects indicated which lines were of matching length

        a.   If even one of the confederates gave an incorrect answer, participants conformed most of
                the time.
        b.   If three or more confederates gave incorrect answers, participants conformed most of the
                time.
        c.   If three or more confederates gave incorrect answers, participants conformed
                approximately ½ of the time.
        d.   If at least one confederate gave a different answer than the others, participants followed
                their own judgments most of the time.

15.   If an adolescent shoplifts in order to be like her friends, her friends represent a

    a.   positive influence
    b.   negative reference group
    c.   positive reference group
    d.   social-emotional leader

16.   The group member who tries to keep the group working cohesively, with minimum animosity, is referred to as the

    a.   autocratic leader
    b.   laissez-faire leader
    c.   tension-release leader
    d.   social-emotional leader

17.   Zimbardo's research in which students played roles of prison inmates and guards showed that

    a.   roles can actually influence social behavior
    b.   because the roles were hypothetical, the students did not take them seriously
    c.   roles have little influence on social behavior
    d.   social behavior likely affects the roles people choose

18.   In Kurt Lewin's study where groups of boys made crafts after school, the style of leadership that led to efficiency but also discontent was a _____ style.

    a.   autocratic
    b.   democratic
    c.   laissez-faire
    d.   permissive

19.   The personality dimensions characteristic of successful leaders are

    a.   extroversion and stubbornness
    b.   extroversion, risk-taking, and friendliness
    c.   persuasiveness, meekness, and cheerfulness
    d.   extroversion, agreeableness, conscientiousness

20.   The technique of intentionally making a request that we know will be turned down, so that when we back down from our request, the other individual should reciprocate our concession is known as:

    a.   low-balling
    b.   the foot-in-the-door technique
    c.   the door-in-the-face technique
    d.   social loafing

ANSWERS

FILL-IN EXERCISES

1. altruism 2. reciprocal 3. matching 4. passionate; companionate 5. females 6. ethical hedonism
7. reciprocal altruism 8. diffusion 9. instrumental 10. hypothalamus 11. testosterone 12. unpleasant
13. violent 14. cause; desensitize 15. unstable 16. influence 17. authority 18. conformity 19. reference
20. role 21. task leader 22. facilitation 23. loafing 24. laissez-faire 25. low-balling

APPLICATION

1. *Conformity*. As in Asch's studies on judgments of line length, this situation involves an individual who is confronted with opinions that differ from hers. Jan likes Ruth. But her classmates agree that it's not cool to like Ruth. So Jan changes her opinion to conform to the group.

2. What led to it was amount of opposition and need for social approval. Jan is a new student who wants to be accepted into her new peer group. Because her classmates unanimously agree that it's not cool to be Ruth's friend, Jan suppresses her opinion that Ruth is her friend, and conforms to the group opinion to gain their approval.

3. Yes. In Asch's studies, if even one confederate allied himself with the subject, the participants were more likely to stick with their original opinion. If one classmate had stood up for Ruth, it is likely that Jan would have stuck to her original opinion about Ruth.

4. A *norm*. All groups develop norms, or standards for behavior. This group of girls has an unspoken standard that it is not cool to be seen with Ruth.

5. The group is a *positive* reference group because Jan tries to emulate its members and meet their standards.

SAMPLE TEST QUESTIONS

1.	a	11.	b
2.	b	12.	b
3.	d	13.	c
4.	a	14.	d
5.	d	15.	c
6.	c	16.	d
7.	d	17.	a
8.	b	18.	a
9.	c	19.	d
10.	a	20.	c